"A well thought and very informative expose of e-commerce, this book is a must read for all who must understand where the technology of the internet is taking business and human interactions."

—Abdel Aziz El-Aguizy, Chairman & CEO, www.quinsys.net and chairman of www.speedsend.com, an Egyptian B2B company providing online officesupplies to large businesses

"Dr. McCue's book dispels all the myths that still pervade e-commerce and offers a practical, thorough, informative guide on how to do business online. The most persistent questions about e-commerce are 'Where do I begin' (from Internet neophytes) and 'How can I make it work better for my business?' This book answers both in full, and it's the best resource out there to answer those questions and others."

—David Berkowitz, former Editor, eMarketer, and Director of Marketing, icrossing

"Jumping into the world of e-commerce is just like jumping into the world of regular commerce: very intimidating. However, in some ways it is even more difficult, because so many of the rules are new or shifting and because our human instincts about 'what to do' and 'where to turn' do not so easily apply in the virtual, digital world. Dr. McCue has provided a great map to this virtual e-commerce world—providing the context, 'rules', examples, and hints that, in my opinion, can dramatically up your odds of success. This excellent book is well worth the investment even for that reason alone."

—James P. Clark, Chairman, The World Technology Network (www.wtn.net)

"The next decade provides a unique window for making innovative investments which can make a lasting difference for the billions untouched by new technologies. Wealth creation, not poverty alleviation has to be the new mantra. E-commerce holds much promise for the developing world and by building creative partnerships and alliances we can enable those who do not have a voice to be heard. Sarah McCue is right on target with her efforts to strengthen this critical field."

—Amir A. Dossal, Executive Director, United Nations Fund for International Partnerships

"Sarah McCue is an inspirational international leader, able to communicate complex concepts in a clear and precise manner, someone who by her charisma, presence and gravitas is able to relate to youth both in the developed and developing worlds. Her experience is multi-cultural, equally at ease in the corridors of the United Nations in Geneva passionately arguing for funds in favor of the emerging world as in an African village coaching youth on how to make use of available technology so as to reduce the unacceptable and discriminating digital gap. While her experience has primarily evolved in the not-for-profit and humanitarian environments, Sarah McCue is an entrepreneur at heart, someone with a keen business sense and a deep belief that people- and trade-exchanges are means to make ours a better world. Her research and analysis on e-commerce, reflected in this publication, is her significant contribution to attaining this desirable goal."

—Victor H. Loewenstein, Retired Partner, Egon Zehnder International

"Dr. McCue provides a broad overview of e-commerce, with something for everyone—consumers, businesses, governments and international organizations. She primarily provides a "developed world" perspective, yet casts a thoughtful eye on some of the international implications and highlights issues for consideration by developing countries. The book also includes concepts and policy issues as well as advice for businesses and organizations wanting to embark on e-commerce. A good introduction for many readers!"

—Mohamed Muhsin, Vice President and Chief Information Officer, World Bank

"Brilliant and comprehensive! This book is truly a fresh approach about the e-commerce process. It is packed with great tips for developing countries. Congratulations to Dr. McCue."

—Renata Sanches, Project manager, Brazilian Export Promotion Agency-APEX Brasil

"Here is a thought-provoking, culturally sensitive and global in coverage practical guide on e-commerce. A must for all interested in e-commerce."

—Chetan Sharma—Founder, Datamation Foundation Trust (India) www.datamationfoundation.org

"Dr. McCue does an excellent job in providing an overall roadmap to e-ecommerce and making sense of the Internet as a business and marketing medium. She not only raises the appropriate questions on how to make sense of e-commerce—'is it more hype than hope?'—but also offers valuable insights and checklists for developing a successful e-commerce strategy and creating effective e-commerce Web sites. A definite 'must read' for anyone considering or currently executing an e-business strategy!"

—James Van Wert, DPA; Senior Advisor for Policy Planning and E-Government, U.S. Small Business Administration, Washington, DC

Farce to Force

Building Profitable
E-Commerce Strategies

Sarah S. McCue, Ph.D.

AMERICAN MARKETING ASSOCIATION

THOMSON ™

Australia · Brazil · Canada · Mexico · Singapore · Spain · United Kingdom · United States

Farce to Force: Building Profitable E-Commerce Strategies
Sarah S. McCue

In honor of Saint Isidore of Seville, Patron Saint of the Internet, proposed by the Vatican in November, 2001. Saint Isidore is attributed with writing the world's first encyclopedia, known as Etymologia. Written in 600 A.D., it is a twenty-volume collection of writings on subjects ranging from art, medicine, history, and theology to mathematics, literature, agriculture, war and mineralogy.

If information is power, organized information that is globally available is revolutionary. Thus, let us use this information to bridge the digital divide and create economic opportunity in all countries.

For Elise and Miriam

Think deeply; love widely

CONTENTS

E-Commerce:
Force or Farce?

Since the introduction of the first commercial sites in 1994, e-commerce has spread across the globe as a marketing, sales, and communication phenomenon, even totally changing the face of some business sectors. As a result, new uses and users of the Internet have grown faster than for any other technology in history. Between 1993 and 1997, the number of computers connected to the Internet rose from one to 20 million. By 2007, this figure is expected to reach 1.35 billion. To capitalize on such large numbers of people using the Internet, investment markets were quick to embrace e-commerce as a financially viable medium for B2B (business-to-business) and B2C (business-to-consumer) trade. Equally enthusiastically, enterprises around the world sought to use the Internet to increase their marketing reach and improve their profitability.

There is no question that the Internet has provided greater access to technical and practical information and to lowered communication costs. It has also facilitated access to local, national, and foreign business and consumer markets and thus increased competition as well as sales. In many instances, this has contributed to higher-quality products and lower prices for consumers. Some sectors are thriving on the Internet. As of the end 2003, the strongest growth in B2B and B2C e-commerce was in services such as finance, education, entertainment, software, and retail products, such as clothing, shoes, processed foods, and health products. Yet, in some instances, it has also reduced profit margins for businesses.

Changing Consumer and Buyer Psychology: Shoving a Square Peg into a Round Hole?

Why, as Forrester Research shows, did retail sales total just $12.5 billion, or 1.5 percent of all retail sales from April through June, 2003, even though the percentage was up from 1.2 percent in the same quarter of 2002 (http://www.Forrester.com)? Why did B2B and B2C transactions account for just 1.6 percent of sales in the fourth quarter of 2002 in the United States, even though that is up from 0.7 percent in all of 1999? Why have thousands and thousands of dot.bombs imploded since 2002? Why are others not reaching their expected return on investment?

Because designing and maintaining Web sites is being unnecessarily complicated by those who are unfamiliar with using the Internet as a sales and marketing medium. And because changing the buyer, supplier and consumer mentality and orientation is difficult—but not impossible. It was one thing to move shopping habits from the bazaar to a store. It's quite another to change habits from a store to the Internet—and too many sites are not making it easy.

Think about how frustrated you become when using the Internet—when:

- You can't find what you want using search engines.
- Nobody returns your e-mail inquiries or, worse yet, when you can't find an e-mail address when you have a question that is not addressed in a "Frequently Asked Questions" set up.
- It is difficult to find the price of a product or the shipping costs.
- You don't know if it is safe to provide your credit card number.
- You have to enter identical information for shipping and billing rather than type "same."
- You don't know when or how a product will be shipped.
- You don't receive a confirmation of your order, along with the seller's identifying number, by e-mail.
- You cannot easily find the status of your order.
- The pictures of a part of a product don't show you what you need to know.
- Technical specifications are buried deep within the site.

And this appears to be just the beginning: These are just some of the constraints we continue to identify in our research.

Often it's just easier to pick up the phone and call, instead of trying to conduct business online. After all, at the end of the day, we are human beings who like to talk to other human beings, touch things that we will bring into our workplaces and homes, and ask questions in a human interchange called dialogue between the customer and the business.

We have to ask ourselves the serious question of whether the Internet really *is* going to be a significant sales and marketing tool for millions of small businesses, an efficient parts-to-production-and-distribution system for only a few sectors, such as online auctions, apparel, flowers, video, travel, music, books, and news. Or will it ever become significant for a huge array of products and services. Are we trying to shove a square peg (e-commerce and Information and Communications Technology [ICT]) into a round hole (traditional buying practices)? Or are we working hard to make changes so that the edges are softened and there is a smooth, seamless blend of traditional and e-commerce practices? It's up to the designers and managers to be smart about this transition.

Understanding e-commerce and information and communication technology isn't rocket science. The Internet is a new tool that, if understood, could help businesses improve their productivity, customer service, and expand into new markets. But often even the media are confused by what is happening in the Internet marketplace. Technology developers insist on creating smaller, better, faster, and more gadgets, gizmos, and software, yet most of us can't program our cell phones to receive attachments that we don't really want to receive in the first place. Researchers and professors often study off-track and esoteric issues. Businesses are building unprofitable sites because they aren't listening or responding to their customers and/or don't know how to use information and telecommunication technology. And too many buyers have either tuned out or only use a few giant sites, such as Amazon.com or eBay, for their e-commerce.

Great Expectations

We've heard it all before. The hype. The hope. Developing a site will expand exports into new foreign markets! Buyers around the world will find your site and buy from you! Participate in an e-marketplace and increase sales! Create efficiencies in your business using CRM, ERM, and database management software!

To implement an e-procurement system, you "simply" need an application server, commerce platform, content manager, customer service application, enterprise portal server, e-procurement application, integration server, and marketing automation. Use content management software that allows companies to integrate database systems and share information with suppliers, customers, and employees, efficiently store and effectively retrieve documents, and shorten requisition approval processes. It all sounds so logical.

And this was the hype millions believed until untold thousands went from "dot.com" to "dot.bomb" in March 2001.

The greatest of expectations was followed by uncertainty, doubt, confusion, frustration, chaos, disintegration, analysis, and, slowly, recovery. But has the Internet matured into an understandable sales, marketing, customer support, and efficiency-creating medium? Have we learned from our mistakes? Will there ever be an e-business model? Is the Internet and ICT simply a way to do business better, more efficiently, more effectively?

Thousands of myths and misperceptions still permeate the charred landscape. Forrester Research, eMarketer, IDC Research, Gartner Group, and Jupiter Research are but a few firms spending millions of dollars to understand, create, and promote an e-commerce business model.

F---edCompany.com: What Were They Thinking?

There is much more to understand than just technology and customer service, however, about why e-commerce is growing only in certain sectors. As of March of 2001, of 573 Internet companies that went public in a two-year time frame, 43 percent are doing poorly, trading at US$5 a share or less. In 2000, Toys.com was trading at US$83 a share and in May, 2001, the company declared bankruptcy. Clearly, we need to understand the Internet much more than any of us do at this time. Technical talk is not enough. Much, much more analysis is needed.

Despite it's offensive name, f---edCompany.com is an excellent site that lists the thousands of dot.coms that continue to shut down or businesses that are in trouble. It gives a fascinating glimpse as to what lies abandoned on the information superhighway.

They include ComputerWare.com, a site that sold Macintosh computers; an insurance portal; a financial advising site; extreme championship wrestling; NBCi.com; idolls.com; stamps.com; CDWorld.com; fishoil.com; calendarcentral.com; freestuff.com; jobs.com; and urbancool.com wherein US$23 million was invested to provide free Internet access in urban areas.[3] Ipublish.com raised US$10 million in investment funds, but its electronic book publishing service is now defunct. Powertrust.com was an online electricity broker, and is now US$10–50 million in debt.

Jancentral.com raised US$7 million to sell janitorial supplies online and was restructuring in 2002.

Why did they close their sites? Was it lack of financing, a poorly conceived and implemented idea, lack of systems integration, inadequate marketing strategy, or all of the above—or something else? If these sites cannot survive, then which can?

In the US, only about 35 percent of enterprises use the Internet to sell products or buy supplies. According to a 2002 report from the National Association of Purchasing Management and Forrester Research, *E-Commerce: Exploiting the B2B Model*, companies in the US are only now beginning to move their procurement online. Almost half of the companies in the survey said they were in the earliest stage of using the Internet for purchasing. The larger organizations were more likely to have purchased online and to have experienced major benefits from doing so, and 27 percent claimed they had actually saved money. The percentage of business carried out this way was still small, with only 6 percent of the companies completing more than 40 percent of their purchasing online.

Just look at a few of the headlines that trumpeted new developments, research, and findings made in 2002 (see Exhibit 1.1). It is a brief but interesting snapshot of the diverse and interwoven issues that are important to any e-commerce strategy. They are an indication of just how wide and how deep are the problems and evolving solutions.

Clearly e-commerce questions, technology applications, and markets are maturing as evidenced by the tone and focus of research articles. No longer are researchers blindly watching the e-commerce market unfold as they did in the mid- to late 1990s. Research is continuing and expanding, but it is blended with a level-headed mix of optimism, pragmatism, and sometimes outright skepticism (Exhibit 1.2). Overall, the tone is positive, upbeat, and the focus is on a profitable future.

Making Sense of It

Despite even the new-found focus and more clearly defined purpose, however, most Internet businesses are still not turning a profit. In fact, only in the first quarter of 2002 did Amazon.com finally post a US$5 million profit compared to the firm reporting a net loss of US$545 million in the same quarter of 2001. How did Amazon.com finally avoid hitting the iceberg, having hung by its fingernails since starting its site in July 1995?

Why are only 17 percent of businesses surveyed by Jupiter Communications satisfied with the performance of their site?

Exhibit 1.1 Headlines: The Hope

Automotive: Distribution, Suppliers, and Retail
OnStar Bets Smart on Safety Enhancements
New ASPs Break Auto Repair Bottlenecks
Connecting Dealership Computing

Consumer Devices and Services: Broadband, Consumer Electronics, Devices
Hispanic Households Embrace Tech Devices
eTolls Encounter Privacy Roadblocks
Consumer Trust Is a Core Nokia Asset

Consumer Packaged Goods: Merchandising, Distributors, Logistics, and Retail
Effective E-Mail Marketing for CPG Manufacturers
Cutting the Fat Out of CPG Logistics
Mastering CPG Direct Sales
Collaborating for CPG Success

Content Management: Web Content, Enterprise Content, and Digital Assets
The New Knowledge Management Landscape
Enterprise Content Management Delusions
How to Get Buy-In For Content Management

Customer Relationship Management: Sales, Marketing & Service, Call Centers, and E-Mail
Lands' End Makes Online Chat a Success
Mastering Online Customer Service
Making CRM Multilingual

Enterprise Applications: ERP, Enterprise Services Automation, and B2B Sell-Side
Resolving Conflict over ISVs' Services Revenues
Enterprise Apps Need an Exchange Infrastructure
SAP's Experience Typifies State of E-Government

Infrastructure: Portals, Servers, Corporate Wireless, and Storage
Software Innovations Shift to Platforms and Portfolios
Making Your Portal Mobile
How to Evaluate Business Intelligence Platforms
Enough, Already! Storage Vendors Must Share APIs

Integration and Web Services: Middleware and EAI/B2B Integration Tools
How to Buy an Integration Server
The Right Way to Manage Business Processes
The Web Services Payoff

Marketing: Branding, Promotion, and Cross-Media Marketing
Moving Consumers with Effective Touchpoints
Connecting to Consumers Who Don't Click
Segment Consumers Using Technographics Data
Making Marketing Measurable

Networks and Security: Enterprise Network Management, Equipment, and Services
The Easiest Way to Improve IT Security
New Strategies for Virus Protection
New FTC Privacy Plan Makes Life Harder For Firms

Procurement and Sourcing: Purchasing, Supplier Management, and Marketplaces
Which Manufacturers Succeed at Online Buying?
Banks Must Partner to Offer Source-To-Pay

Retail
Which Retail Product Display Tools Matter Most
Retailers' E-mail Marketing Challenge
Paying with RFID, Smart Cards, and Biometrics
Boost Margins with Merchandise Optimizations

Services: ASPs, Hosting, Outsourcing, and Systems Integrators
Transforming Outsourcing with Organic IT
The Audit-Consulting Split
Distributed Projects Give Pivotal Providers a Lift

Supply Chain: Planning & Execution, Logistics, and Product Design
The Collaborative Product Life Cycle
Intercompany Change Fuels Post-Recession Growth
Opening the Logistics Black Box

Technology Leadership: Budgeting, Organization, Staffing, and Partnerships
Six New Technologies to Boost Business Results
Tech Buyers Must Balance Product Capabilities Against Vendor Strength
Reinventing Technology Management

Source: Headlines exerpted from news articles posted on http://www.forrester.com.

Exhibit 1.2 Research Findings from Forrester Research (FR) and *Internet Weekly* (IW)

IW January 2002 Tight IT budgets and higher-than-expected integration costs are slowing the growth of private exchanges, but early adopters say they're not altering plans for expansion.

IW January 2002 Cyberattack activity increased 79% among 300 companies surveyed between July and December last year by security-services vendor Riptech Inc. Some industries are more attack prone than others, says the report.

FR Jan 07 2002 Only 30 percent of online retailers responded to customer service e-mail requests within six hours during the holiday shopping season, according to Jupiter Media Metrix.

FR Jan 17 2002 Forty-five percent of large-volume-buying organizations in the US polled in Q4 2001 said that buying online saves them money, according to Forrester Research and the Institute for Supply Management.

FR 25 January 2002 130 million Europeans will play mobile games by 2005 if the industry can move past today's broken business models. Operators must track and share revenues while marketers sponsor branded games.

FR 30 January 2002 Retailers must use technology to regain sales momentum in 2002. Those that master technology to optimize product assortments and prices, integrate online and offline operations, and embrace standards to facilitate collaboration will gain market share.

IW 31 January 2002 According to the Moscow Times, 9 percent of all Russians use computers several times a week, at home, at work, or elsewhere.

MSNBC 05 February 2002 143 million people, or 54 percent of the total population, are now online in the US, up 26 percent from last year.

FR 6 February 2002 ElectricNews.Net reports that there will be 130 million wireless gamers in Europe by 2005, up from the present figure of 5 million.

FR 6 February 2002 According to a new study from DoubleClick, almost half of European marketers use online marketing tools. UK marketers are most likely to engage in online marketing, as 73 percent do so. Sixty-six percent of Spanish marketers use online marketing tools, as do 43 percent of German marketers, 34 percent of Scandinavian marketers, 31 percent of those in Italy, and 21 percent of those in France. E-mail marketing is the most popular form of online marketing in Europe, used by 31 percent of marketers. Targeted banners are used by 27 percent, and newsletters by 24 percent.

FR 12 February 2002 Almost 32 percent of Chinese Internet users bought goods or services online in 2001, according to the China Internet Network Information Center.

IW 12 February 2002 Kalido Ltd. continues to build momentum as a provider of business integration software that helps companies integrate operations following a merger.

Are smaller businesses selling products and services on the Internet or is it dominated by large businesses?

What is the average ratio of "hits" (the number of visits to a site) to leads to sales of most sites? Obviously, creating a well-designed, high traffic site is not as simple as was once expected. What, then, are the essential elements of a winning site?

No wonder enterprises around the globe question if it is worth their staff's time to design and maintain a fully functional and expensive site or participate in an e-marketplace.

Thousands of enterprises still ask these questions as the Internet evolves into a marketing medium that some day may be as common as advertising in the newspaper, at a trade show, or in a trade journal. The Internet is an ever-changing, relatively new marketing medium that confuses, frustrates, and yet gives hope to millions of enterprises attempting to penetrate new markets. The answers to many of these questions can be found in the following chapters. And more answers and more questions will keep on evolving as the use of the Interest improves and evolves.

Scores of articles have been written regarding the explosion in the use of the Internet. However, actual research into propensity for consumers to use the Internet to purchase products and services, successful e-marketing techniques, analysis of "hits to sales" levels, and overall constraints of e-commerce is sparse. In fact, the limited research that has been conducted shows that the Internet has not proven to be very successful at increasing sales for medium and small businesses.

So, how does one make sense of it all?

We have several more years to go before the Internet is organized efficiently and technology is affordable and practical for e-commerce. And it will be longer than that for buyers and consumers to reorient fully and completely their traditional buying practices, psychology, and thinking to use the Internet for their everyday needs. This is true for all countries, especially the United States, often viewed as the epicenter and leader of e-commerce.

Myths and Misperceptions Regarding E-Commerce and ICT

Here are just some of the phenomena that affect business thinking:

- Believing that every business should be an e-commerce business.

- Believing that having a site will increase sales.
- Believing that the Internet is an easy way to make one's business and products known worldwide. In 2005 there were over 8 billion pages visible and searchable on the World Wide Web, and the number is growing exponentially. Being present on the Web does not mean being visible.
- Believing that an e-commerce strategy supercedes and/or replaces the firm's overall strategy.
- Not spending enough to promote the site by registering with search engines, direct mail, using e-mail messaging, and using print, television and other traditional methods to *show* customers how to use the site.
- Not realizing that it is difficult to change consumer and buyer psychology, and to force them into your e-commerce strategy.
- Not spending enough time on the site's content, layout, and navigation; not using technology for integration within the firm and among customers. Many enterprises lose customers because the site is difficult to use, and the technology is too advanced.
- Not having someone in the firm to contact.
- Not responding quickly to customer requests for information sent via e-mail.
- Designing a site that makes it difficult for customers to identify the advantages of the product.
- Building a site that makes it difficult for customers to buy from the firm.
- Not updating the site frequently.
- No strong involvement of intermediaries or middlemen. Many manufacturers are not equipped and are not willing to deal with the individual firm or person ordering a product, and yet have not devised a solution to integrate middlemen into cyberspace.

If you are a manager of an e-business, ask yourself: Are you satisfied with the performance or return on the investment of your site? Have you made a purchase online in the last month? Do you buy your supplies online? Are the various departments or functions of your business integrated for increased efficiency and sharing of information? Do you know the types of software programs that will automate your business? Is your software integrated within your company? Can you share files between your buyers and suppliers? Does your business use enterprise resource planning (ERP) software along with customer (CRM), partner

(PRM), and employee relationship management (ERM) software to create a holistic systems management plan supported by an enterprise application integration software? Of course not, and mine does not either. This is my point.

What Site Characteristics Worked and What Didn't: A Comparison of North American and European Sites

The Enterprise Directorate General of the European Commission conducted a survey of business sites in 1999 to determine general characteristics of business sites. The study involved the collection of information on more than 200,000 business-to-business sites. Some 2,129 site owners were asked to comment on their enterprise's site design, Internet strategy, and expectations of marketing on the Internet.

The study found that the most sites served four business objectives: marketing, sales, customer service, and interfirm communication. Initial expectations, including the development of new business specifically for the Web and interaction between departments in the company and customers, distributors and suppliers, were not met.

The businesses experienced an increased penetration in international markets, replaced existing print and television advertisements with Internet marketing techniques, improved their customer service using information and communication technology, and increased the overall brand awareness. These benefits were realized with low expenditure and minimum allocation of personnel for the site.

The study also found that senior managers, such as the general manager, sales manager, or marketing manager, contributed greatly to the success of the Internet strategy instead of relying upon a chief information officer to integrate disparate ideas from various divisions or sections of the company.

More than 85 percent of the North American sites surveyed were monolingual. In contrast, 32 percent of the European sites were available in two or more languages.

Almost half of the sites comprised just a few pages (under 10), and more than half of the companies updated these pages at least once a month.

Just over half of the companies used some form of paid promotion for their sites, while eight percent said they did not promote their site at all.

In terms of payment methods, about a third of the North American sites accepted payment by credit card, while-only 18 percent of the European sites did so.

The study also found that Europeans did not use their sites for sales as much as the North Americans did. Around 90 percent of the sites that were used for customer service and support claimed to respond to customer queries within a day.

More than three-quarters of the site owners were satisfied with the results of their site, while 22 percent said they got less than expected. Nearly two-thirds of the companies surveyed increased their product turnover because of their sites, mostly as a result of direct or indirect sales. Two-thirds said there was only a moderate increase (0 percent to 25 percent), but one-tenth said they increased their turnover by more than 50 percent.

Well over half of the companies surveyed saved money because of their site, mostly in reductions in telecommunications, mailings, and office supplies and expenses.

A Force or Farce?

In light of the myths and misperceptions and the difficulties that millions of firms face when trying to implement a profitable e-commerce strategy, will e-commerce evolve into a mature force that is responsible for a third or half of all sales, or will it remain misunderstood by the media, studied by academics, pushed by software developers, and ignored by smaller businesses?

Hope abounds, but so does hype. Whether the Internet is a force or a farce for you is up to you.

2

The E-Commerce Challenge Faced by Enterprises Around the World

It is obvious that there is vast opportunity to expand the number of business-to-business (B2B), business-to-consumer (B2C), and business-to-government (B2G) transactions. Consider, for example, the revenue potential indicated in Exhibit 2.1.

The challenge is not to understand that there is potential for e-commerce, but to propose innovative, cost effective, and results-based solutions, because there is vast, vast untapped potential to survive and thrive in the global electronic economy.

Learning to Survive and Thrive in the E-conomy

How can enterprises design profitable e-commerce/ICT strategies? Scores of articles and books have been written regarding the exploding use of the Internet and what marketing, sales, information, communication, systems integration, and other technology will ensure success. However, actual research is sparse regarding how consumers use the Internet to purchase products and services, successful e-marketing techniques, analysis of "hits to sales" levels, and overall constraints of e-commerce.

Therefore, to identify the contemporary constraints and needs facing businesses, I approached a cross section of businesses, decision-makers, private and not-for-profit organizations, government representatives, and experts in the field of e-commerce to better understand the

EXHIBIT 2.1 Actual and Projected B2C E-Commerce Revenues by World Region

Region	2000	2001	2002	2003	2004
North America	47.5	74.4	110.6	135.3	197.9
Latin America	0.7	1.8	3.3	5.5	8.1
Europe	8.1	16.5	37.1	81.8	182.5
Africa/Mid East	0.2	0.3	0.6	1.1	1.6
Asia	3.2	8.3	15.6	26.4	38
World	59.7	101.1	167.2	250	428.1

Source: eMarketer 2001, www.emarketer.com

important marketing, technological, infrastructural, strategic, political, socioeconomic, legal, and other issues facing enterprises.

Several surveys were undertaken in 1999 and later: (1) an electronic survey of selected firms in February, (2) an electronic survey of selected trade support institutions in March, (3) a telephone survey of trade ministers, and (4) an electronic survey of key private sector decision-makers in the field of e-commerce. In addition, a focus group of individuals from missions representing countries with a strong interest in the area of electronic commerce was held at the United Nations' International Trade Center (ITC) in Geneva in April. Furthermore, a review of primary and secondary research was compiled to identify the important research conducted recently in the field of e-commerce.

A summary of this research follows. It outlines the unique needs facing businesses as they attempt to capitalize on the opportunities inherent in this emerging sales and marketing medium.

The E-Commerce Challenge: Constraints and Barriers

Barriers to electronic commerce development by enterprises can be characterized by the following:

Cost

Many enterprises find that the actual cost of setting a business on the Internet is much higher than originally anticipated. This is due to misunderstanding Internet marketing, a lack of training, management time spent deciding on Internet marketing strategies, time spent with graphic designers who design and update the site, and overall lack of funds to design a site. Research consistently has shown that retailers and manufacturers face cost constraints on the allocation of financial and human resources for their site development and frequent updates.

In addition to the cost of basic computer hardware and software, the cost of using the Internet depends on the price of router services and charges of ISPs. In addition to the fee to design a basic site, the monthly maintenance fee, and basic Internet access, there are significant costs for research, development, staffing, and promotion.

Security

Although some feel that the technological aspects of ensuring security in online transactions has largely been solved (e.g., authentication, non-repudiation, integrity of data and integrity of system, and confidentiality), security issues remain vitally important for enterprises using electronic commerce in terms of customer fraud, the potential for hackers to gain access to vulnerable information, and the security of ISPs.

Lack of Success

According to the US Department of Commerce (http://www.stat-usa. gov/), e-commerce sales in the second quarter of 2002 accounted for 1.2 percent of total sales, while in the second quarter of 2001, e-commerce sales were 1.0 percent of total sales. Despite the global hype and hope, this hard statistic reveals that e-commerce has a long, long way to go before it replaces traditional commerce as a significant means of conducting business. Yet worldwide competition on the Internet is growing rapidly. According to its home page on the following dates, Google searched 4,285,188,744 Web pages on June 5, 2004, and 8,058,044,651 Web pages on April 26, 2005.

Lack of Business E-Commerce Strategy

Many enterprises find it difficult to design a site with truly useful information for clients. Enterprises that don't understand how to list products and services predominantly with search engines remain lost in the haystack, impossible to find by new or existing customers. Crafting a winning strategy involves a unified, integrated, and shared vision among employees, customers, and suppliers. Without this e-commerce strategy, firms will be disappointed by the low level of visits to the Web site relative to the company's investment in it.

Lack of National E-Commerce Strategies

Government agencies, nonprofit organizations, and national associations, etc., must grapple with a number of financial, legal, connectivity, and other policy issues related to e-commerce. These include issues of encryption, security of payments, taxation, certification and authentication, privacy, intellectual property protection, fraud and consumer protection, and access to telecommunications. Such a national e-commerce strategy must also address how the Internet will benefit enterprises, foster an awareness and appreciation among enterprises of what the Internet is, provide answers to technical and security questions, and train enterprises on how to use the Internet as a sales, marketing, communication, and supply management medium.

Thus, these groups need to foster policies and programs to increase the overall number of enterprises using the Internet by enterprises focusing on integrated electronic access to information, access to electronic education and training, electronic access to network of buyers and suppliers, and access to electronic transactions for obtaining a loan online, ordering suppliers, and paying taxes. It is indeed remarkable that the US government has no overall strategy to create these types of programs and services to allow their entrepreneurs to better thrive and survive using e-commerce and ICT.

Lack of Support in Business Assistance

In the majority of countries, there is lack of overall support by business development organizations to help businesses with their e-commerce strategy. The lack of adequate and contemporary counseling, training, research, and support is a significant constraint for thousands of businesses wanting to transact business between their respective countries.

Limited Use of Internet to Locate and Buy Products and Services

E-mail and marketing to new customers are the predominate uses of Internet by enterprises. In 1998, I found through my independent research that only 1.4 percent of Internet use among enterprises and consumers is toward the actual purchase of goods and services. In 2002, according to *Wired News*, this figure rose to 1.6 percent.

Based on these studies and the disparities in percentages among the studies, it is clear that conclusions regarding the use and importance of the Internet are still difficult to determine. The point is that in 2005 e-commerce is in its infancy and is not as important to businesses—yet—as one would expect. The bottom line implications are that the majority of businesses have not yet adopted and integrated technology to facilitate more e-commerce transactions, and that perhaps the majority of consumers and buyers are more comfortable with offline purchasing.

Note that the US Small Business Administration (SBA) expected business-to-business e-commerce in the United States to grow from US$17 billion in 1998 to US$327 billion in 2001. The SBA also expected business-to-consumer (B2C) online shopping would rise from US$2.4 billion in 1997 to US$17.4 billion in 2001. This indicates that B2B transactions are expected to be 17 times greater than B2C purchasing.

In fact, according to the US Department of Commerce, B2B transactions accounted for US$777 billion in 2000, an increase of seven percent over US$730 billion in e-shipments, with B2C online shopping having reached US$29 billion in 2000.

Lack of Knowledge and Application of Information Technology

Research of enterprises has consistently shown that awareness of how to apply information and communication technologies to their operations is limited. From the most senior to junior level employee, modern work skills are needed in basic understanding of hardware and e-commerce software, designing basic Web sites, processing electronic payments, etc.

Although the situation is improving, most enterprises from Australia to Zimbabwe do not possess a widely skilled workforce to address these issues. If a shift in thinking and action is ever to occur, universities must reorient their curriculum, technical schools must provide much more hands-on e-commerce and ICT training, and government-funded organizations such as Small Business Development Centers must offer a national certificate program on electronic commerce for enterprises.

Conflict with Buyers' and Consumers' Traditional Buying Practices

Buyers want to comparison shop, find good quality pictures of products that are described well, and ask questions and get answers online in a quick and secure fashion. Yet many find themselves unable to talk with

---

EXHIBIT 2.2 Types of 21st-Century Technology That Businesses and Organizations Must Understand . . . and Use

---

- Enterprise Resource Planning software/interlinked software/pioneered by SAP.
- Enterprise Application Integration software/connects PCs and software systems/led by CrossWorlds (IBM), SeeBeyond, Vitira.
- Application Servers/operating system for Web services /BEA, iPlanet, Oracle.
- Customer Relationship Management software/tracks and connects customer, partner and employee data/led by Sibel Systems.
- Partner Relationship Management software/CRM for dealers or distributors.
- Employee Relationship Management software/digitizes and streamlines the "life cycle" of employees' hiring, training, management and retention.
- Systems Management software/technology for monitoring disparate computer systems and networks.

---

someone about a particular product or service, are uncomfortable using credit cards, and want to see the product before purchasing. Many studies consistently find that consumers did not buy online for the following reasons (in priority order):

- Are uncomfortable sending credit card data across the Internet.
- Preferred to see the product before purchasing.
- Couldn't talk to a sales representative.
- Couldn't get enough information to make a decision.
- The product was too expensive relative to alternatives.
- Ordering process took too long.
- Had to download special software.
- Web site was difficult to understand and navigate.
- Process was confusing.
- Product information was not current.

Lack of Adequate Internet Service Providers

While most developed countries have adequate ISP services, the vast majority of the rest of the world do not. In responding to a survey I conducted while at the United Nations International Trade Center on the use of e-commerce by enterprises in developing countries, a representative of the Uganda Export Promotion Board wrote:

> Although electronic commerce is now widely used in developed countries, it is still a new phenomenon in least

developed countries like Uganda. At the moment, we have three companies that are the providers of Internet and e-mail services. The total number of subscribers is 15,000, which is quite insignificant in terms of carrying out viable business. The lack of subscribers is mainly due to the huge amount of money required to purchase computer hardware and software, and the high subscription fees charged by Internet service providers.

Inability to Identify Successful E-Commerce Industries or Sectors

The factors that are driving the decision to create or improve e-commerce capabilities are customer outreach and marketing, increased productivity, and competition. These are all related to reducing the time-to-market factor. In 2002, the industries that were most advanced in responding to these opportunities in the United States were computer and data services, medical, real estate, architectural and other business services, sale of books, music, and autos and parts, auction, insurance, banking, brokerage, and currency trading services, and supplier and subcontractor communications and procurement. However, no research has been conducted to identify which product sectors will likely do well online and which likely won't, based on a criteria of factors.

Inability to Identify What Products Sell Well on the Internet

Intuitively, one could argue that there are products and services better suited to successful Internet sales, marketing, and communication, but conclusive research has not been conducted as to which ones they are. On the other hand, many might argue that *any* type of product or service can be successful. Nevertheless, the following factors are important when attempting to determine which products or services will be easier to sell over the Internet.

Competition. If the product or service is unique, it will fare better on the Internet because of its exclusivity, thus being easier to locate using search engines.

Price. For the majority of online transactions, the bottom line is that, all things being equal, the cheapest price rules the Internet.

The Touch Factor. Consumers still need to touch, see, smell, try on, "kick" (or test), experiment with, or talk to someone about thousands of products.

Uniformity of Product. Those products that are mass manufactured will likely fare better than those that are handmade or custom produced, due to the ability of the manufacturer to produce in volume, which carries a guarantee of consistency of product quality as well as reliability. Consumers are also more likely to be familiar with a mass-produced product.

Immediacy of the Need for a Product. If you need a ladder to change a light bulb, you are likely not going to go to the 'Net to purchase either. On the other hand, retail consumers are likely to order online impulse, non-urgent consumables. Because manufacturers determine production schedules by factoring in time for ordering, shipping, and delivery, they are better suited for the efficiency and effectiveness of the Internet for product ordering and supply management.

Consumer's Understanding of Product. It is reasoned that B2B commerce on the Internet will greatly increase while e-consumer purchases will continue to trickle, except for the largest of firms, such as Amazon.com, Dell and eBay, because manufacturers have a familiarity with product specifications consumer just don't enjoy.

Repeat Usage of Product. Familiar products that need to be purchased on a regular basis (groceries, children's clothing, office supplies, books, etc.) are easier for the consumer to purchase on the Internet to save time and money and relieve boredom. They respond to the immediate need to consume the product.

Consumer Psychology. Not enough research has been conducted on the e-consumer psychology to determine why particular segments of society or business purchase products and services and why they don't. In a survey of 113 firms conducted while I was at Wayne State University in July of 1998, 87 percent indicated that they had not purchased a product or service online in the last six months, and in 2002, 76 percent indicated the same. It appears that consumer and, to a lesser extent, enterprise reluctance to search or purchase products and services online extends far beyond concerns about security of financial transactions. However, limited research has been conducted to identify what these factors are.

EXHIBIT 2.3 What Consumers Buy Online

Books	40 percent
Travel	38 percent
Music CDs or Tapes	30 percent
Computer Software	24 percent
Clothes	21 percent
Event Tickets	18 percent
Toys or Games	16 percent

Source: Scarborough Research www.upsdell.com/BrowserNews/res.design.htm
(Dec. 2000).

Research must also be conducted to identify how to change the consumer psyche and to identify which products or services businesses and consumers will likely purchase online (see Exhibit 2.3). An interesting question: to what extent it is possible to change consumers' and businesses' learned behavior of purchasing?

Perhaps it is easier for businesses to change their mindset to purchase products and services online to reduce costs, improve delivery time, communicate with suppliers, and simply improve efficiencies in order, shipment, and delivery. Or perhaps B2B purchasing is greater because it is so distinctively dissimilar and "faceless" when compared to the traditional consumer experience. It is important to wonder if it is innate to our human nature to want to wander the grand bazaar in Istanbul, the shops in our local downtown, the strip malls, grocery stores, etc. Or does the consumer truly want to spend limited time shopping online to save time for other pursuits such as physical activity or family time?

It is predicted that the major growth sectors in e-commerce and trade will be:

- Global media and entertainment.
- Tourism including hotels and airlines.
- Professional and financial services, insurance, and retailing.

Inability of Governments to Provide Solutions

Typically, governments and trade support institutions are concerned primarily with four facets of e-commerce: (1) integrated electronic access to information (e.g., laws, policies, and regulation compliance tools); (2) access to electronic education and training (Web-based tutorials); (3) electronic access to network (matchmaking buyers and suppliers in equity capital, procurement, trade leads, innovation grants); and (4) access to electronic transactions (e.g., obtaining a loan online, buying a CD, ordering suppliers, paying taxes, etc.).

In connection with these areas, trade support institutions and governments can facilitate the development of programs and services that would be most effective in helping enterprises implement and use electronic commerce. A complete framework illustrating how government can work together with industry is presented in Chapter 9, but the following suggestions are important to note:

- *Identify enterprise e-needs.* Conduct focus groups of large numbers of enterprises to identify needs as they relate to sales, marketing, and communication issues.
- *Identify business and consumer needs.* Conduct research as to why more purchases are not made online and what can be done to encourage more consumer sales and business sales.
- *Identify technological, infrastructural, and political challenges of conducting e-commerce in developing countries.* For example, China, Cuba, and other countries do not allow access to the Internet or e-mail, and in other countries businesses must have their Web site approved by the government prior to allowing Internet customer access.
- *Track usage of Internet.* It is important to understand the growth and slagging areas for B2B and B2C purchases. It is not enough to identify how many businesses or individuals are online or have developed a site to post information. The extent to which business and consumers are using the Internet to purchase goods and services is also important.
- *Track demand of the product within and beyond borders.* Research must be conducted on the extent to which businesses and consumers are seeking products from within the country and outside of it.
- *Determine ROI.* Identify to what extent enterprises are realizing their return on investment (ROI) after having developed a site. Develop case studies of what works, what doesn't, and why. In addition to profiling successful e-marketing strategies, research

must be conducted on the relationship by industry between total site visits, total leads generated, and sales made.

- *Design a tool kit for enterprises.* Include strategies, to put as many enterprises online as well as provide a template for a site that need only be customized by the enterprise.

Organizing the Web for Business

Developed and developing countries should be part of discussions with other countries, private sector search engine firms, and international organizations to better organize the Web for B2B and B2C use. It is imperative that an international business-related search engine be developed, similar to the excellent "private" search engines in the science and technical fields, so that consumers and businesses can easily find the product or service they seek. Until a B2B and B2C search engine is developed, it will be impossible for products and services to be seen among 8 billion Web pages. Businesses and consumers need a well-organized business search engine so that they don't waste time trying to find what they're looking for.

While experimenting trying to find a listing of manufacturers of wool suits, I recently found a poetry site, a family's genealogy, names of bands, movies depicting Fauntleroy suits, the Radio Free Europe site, and IBM Chairman Louis Gerstner's clothing preferences. Of course, Yahoo's and Google's paid search technology helps us find businesses more easily than in the late 1990s, and I could refine and refine my search, but the point is that the Internet is not organized for buyers and suppliers to find each other *easily*. This is the predominate reason why the Internet is not a sales and marketing medium . . . yet.

Exhibits 2.4a and 2.4b provide the results from searches conducted in 2001 and 2005 using different products and different search engines. The first column, "Product" displays the exact format of the words entered for each search. The numbers represent the number of URLs, or Web sites, retrieved by each search engine for the given product.

Clearly the dominant commercial search engines are not adequately organized for buyers to find goods and services on the Internet. Other more specialized business-only search engines are in development, such as UDDI, or Universal Description, Discovery and Integration, a white pages business directory and a technical specifications library. However, the search engines are being used for sourcing by only a

EXHIBIT 2.4a Search Engine Searches, 2001

Product	Alta Vista	Excite	Google	Lycos	Infoseek
silk ties	6,473	900	7,673	7,543	4,603
"silk" plus "ties"	449,843	67,455	65,126	53,043	2,170,288
"ties" plus "silk"	629,538	68,970	66,100	53,043	2,170,288
unprocessed fruits	78	62	84	167	45
fruit juices	32,123	1,457	87,323	49,324	27,653
clothing	1,892,495	43,284	4,291,547	5,237,453	982,887
pencils	146,745	12,562	372,581	293,749	1,124,740
handicrafts	129,775	11,365	159,258	123,369	62,963
leather goods	51,713	7,889	122,347	103,874	29,157
book binding	6,437	974	12,765	12,957	7,367
book printing	4,273	856	7,637	12,873	10,756
automotive components	12,986	1,345	13,984	17,223	4,971
pottery	576,237	66,394	763,175	586,491	185,072
graphic design	532,109	713,453	538,463	615,024	283,763
architecture	3,875,373	4,932,392	7,374,733	4,573,953	1,464,901
gold jewelry	29,475	156,845	64,305	59,342	24,970
toys	2,567,472	476,647	5,832,938	7,053,443	2,642,453

Source: McCue; unpublished research, 2001.

EXHIBIT 2.4b Search Engine Searches, 2005

Product	Ask Jeeves	Google	Yahoo
silk ties	71,300	162,000	189,000
unprocessed fruits	19,900	815	577
clothing	50.140	125,000,000	100,000,000
pencils	2,013,000	6,270,000	5,840,000
handicrafts	938,300	2,770,000	2,530,000
leather goods	2,315,000	948,000	1,870,000
book printing	185,900	176,000	278,000
automotive components	2,384,000	170,000	261,000
pottery	12,500,000	15,800,000	21,500,000
graphic design	13,780,000	22,800,000	25,700,000
architecture	32,470,000	211,000,000	78,400,000
gold jewelry	9,236,000	868,000	1,830,000
toys	98,260,000	79,200,000	129,000,000

Source: McCue; unpublished research, 2005.

fraction of the world's businesses. In the future, a widely-known business search engine for *all* types of products and services in *all* countries will likely be developed, or registration of business sites will occur within sector-specific portals. Overall organization of the Internet for business purposes should be based on the international Harmonized System or some other internationally recognized protocol.

According to Philippe D. Monnier, president of Eureka Cybertrain, SA in Geneva, Switzerland:

> The Internet phenomenon has generated so much hype, and relevant information is so tightly controlled by the large e-commerce product suppliers, that several die-hard myths have been perpetuated. These myths even seem to gain in importance and lead many decision-makers to wrong decisions.

He further argues that countries must communicate the following truths with their enterprises:

It is not easy for enterprises to make its company and products known worldwide through the Internet. Marketing costs are typically prohibitive.

Intermediaries will not disappear as a result of the e-commerce transaction. Most manufacturers are not equipped and not willing to deal with end-customers.

Internet businesses are not global. Prohibitive marketing costs make them sectoral, local, Intranet, or Extranet-like.

Buzz Words: The Problem with Educators and the Media

The media must be encouraged to print realistic and intelligible articles on e-commerce and information technology. For example, the cover of *Newsweek's* January 29, 2001, issue trumpeted, "Sky High—Forget the Dot-Bombs. The Computer Revolution Is Just Taking Off." However, that is not so for smaller enterprises in general. Most smaller enterprises remain confused about the application and use of information technology in their enterprises, how to design customer-responsive Web sites, and generally how to benefit from this new tool for business organization, communication, marketing, and sales. Smaller enterprises have a multitude of questions on technical issues, crafting e-commerce strategies, protecting privacy, sending electronic signatures and generating

EXHIBIT 2.5 View from an E-Commerce Thought Leader

The Disconnected World of Technologist vs. Manager
Joseph M. Newcomer, President, The Joseph M. Newcomer Co.,
newcomer@flounder.com

We live in an era of technology. Yet many people are functionally illiterate in the technology they are involved with. This becomes apparent in many areas of e-commerce. This is a field in which technology meets business, and the two are inextricably bound. One potential problem is the separation of concerns.

In this corner, we have the technologists. They understand the Internet, routers, IP datagrams, and all those other wonderful terms. They love toys, and they love technology. They wouldn't know a business plan if it came up and bit them on the ankles.

And in this corner, we have have the business types. They understand (we hope!) profit-and-loss, marketing, market positioning, sales, and return-on-investment. Some of them are severely challenged beyond e-mail and simple document production.

These are not good combinations. The technologists will order the top-of-the-line fastest, best, and—and here's the problem—most expensive router, server, Internet connection, etc.

Nobody wants to pay much for the software. The technologists don't want to waste time on incidentals, like an order-fulfillment-and-inventory system (that's for the business types) and therefore don't want to have anything to do with it. The business types have no idea if the technology they are paying for is going to solve their business needs. They don't understand the software either.

Even if you have the best technologists and the best business people, if they don't understand each other's world, you have the potential for major disaster.

In practice, it is far worse. Neophytes in either division are a fatal combination; rarely will a new venture survive this situation.

It is essential that the business people understand the technology. When a technologist comes to them and says "We need a brand X router because it has . . ." the business people will know why a router is important, and be able to force a justification for the expense (perhaps it is the right brand and set of features, but it could be too larger or too small). A US$100,000 capital investment may be exactly the right thing, or it may be horribly incorrect—in either direction! If the technologists don't understand the business plan and the growth plan, they could create a system which does not scale to the needs of the company. Or they could create, for a startup, a system worthy of a long-established multinational corporation.

Technologists must understand business. Business people must understand technology. No, you should not expect your system programmer to develop your detailed marketing plan, and you should not expect your CEO to configure the router (although both could occur!), but they should speak the same language at the interface points where the two worlds meet.

This requires that both sides recognize that they are part of the solution; the technologists cannot live in a technology-only world, nor can the business people implicitly trust the technologists to always do the right thing in the context of the business. Left to themselves, each group will optimize what it is best at. In the e-commerce world, this will not work. The goal is to optimize the business, and that requires serious effort on both sides.

traffic to sites. But glib, confusing and high tech media articles can only delay the fomenting of the revolution.

The media should be encouraged to refrain from the use of complex language and buzz words such as "e-marketplace," "marketspace," "Internet pure plays," "value networks," "response chain," "virtuous circles of productivity gains," "feedback loops," etc., without definitions. More potential consumers and buyers would use the Internet if they understood how to use it. The media should play an important role in educating them and in debunking the myths, misperceptions and myopia surrounding the Internet and related technologies.

Real-Life Experiences with Internet Marketing

Take a close look at the experiences of 15 diverse smaller businesses as they attempted to market and sell on the Internet and use information and communication technology to improve the efficiency and customer service orientation of their businesses. By participating in an intensive research study from 1996 to 1998 at Wayne State University, these US-based smaller businesses learned some valuable lessons on how to survive and thrive on the Internet. They were placed under a microscope for two years. It was a fascinating study, and enterprises in any country should benefit from their Internet experiences detailed below.

Purpose of the Study

In 1996, 15 smaller businesses in a variety of fields were selected by me to study their experiences as they marketed their products and services on the Internet, and attempted to use ICT applications to create efficiencies within their firms. The purpose of the study was to identify the common pitfalls and successes of Internet marketing and ICT, share results with enterprises as they begin to market on the Internet, and help the enterprises decide if the Internet is a wise investment. The study shares their experiences so that enterprises can be more successful than these businesses were in their attempts at implementing an e-commerce strategy.

As part of the project study, sites were designed for these businesses, e-mail accounts were established, training sessions were conducted by e-commerce/ICT experts. The number of visits to the site, number of sales leads generated, and total sales were tracked for the duration of the study.

Optimism and Expectations

The enterprises in this study were optimistic about the seemingly limitless possibilities of the Internet. At the beginning of the study, participants were asked what they expected from Internet and related information and communication technologies. They did not want to design a site simply to attract customers.

Many expected to sell products and services by providing online quotes, advertise in more markets at less expense, use e-mail as a marketing tool, and decrease the costs of printing marketing materials. They also expected to enhance their credibility by projecting a professional image, retain their customers through enhanced efficiency, provide in-depth information by answering questions about products or services in several languages, and conduct foreign market research. Study participants also wanted to improve customer service through use of ICT by offering paperless documentation, improving response time to customer queries, providing same-day service, obtaining feedback from customers. Finally, they wanted to use e-mail as an integral customer care and communication tool. The following are typical expectations.

- Access new customers throughout the world, thus tapping an unexpected market.
- Improve profitability through use of technology; enhance their credibility by projecting a professional online image.
- Decrease customer acquisition costs.
- Advertise in more countries at less expense.
- Reduce the cost of printing.
- Access market information, including current selling prices in various regions, sales activities of competitors, and early identification of industry trends.
- Create the ability for customers to place orders online.
- Answer questions on their products via e-mail.
- Provide technical information online.
- Provide online quotations.
- Improve response time to customer inquiries.
- Obtain feedback from customers for continuous improvement of products and service.

- Post comments from satisfied customers for review by new customers.
- Provide same-day service or service beyond regular office hours.
- Use e-mail as a promotional tool.
- Use e-mail as a customer communications tool.
- Offer paperless documentation.
- Better coordinate the supply chain.
- Conduct foreign market research online.
- Develop a site that responds to a customer's need for information.
- Design a site that is technologically able to achieve these goals.

The firms in the study had a wide range of expectations, on a wide-ranging scale of probability or possibility of realization. Exhibit 2.6 indicates their primary expectations. By identifying their primary expectation, they clarified the way to establish their strategies and proceed with their methods of implementation.

Frustrations

If you compare the number of hits to the number of total leads generated to the total sales made (see Exhibit 2.7), you can conclude that enterprises in this study sold next to nothing on the Internet. Despite the best attempts by e-commerce experts, in-depth training, constant analysis of constraints, use of the most modern technology, and changing of site content and other marketing techniques, the expected return on investment is often not met. Why?

The study revealed that lack of actual sales was due to technological, competency, time, financial, staff, and marketing constraints, all to be covered later. For example, most firms had limited knowledge about how information and communication technologies could contribute to an overall e-commerce strategy. Others were frustrated that they were unable to update the sites—they were too reliant on expensive Web designers and Internet Service Providers (ISPs) who were not responsive to their specific problems or questions. Due to staffing constraints, many firms were frustrated that there was no time to respond to the increase in e-mail and phone inquiries, to use the Internet as a research tool, or to develop and keep the site current.

In terms of marketing constraints, the firms found it challenging to design a site that provides information customers will find useful. Firms were also frustrated that search engines did not list the site prominently,

Exhibit 2.6 Primary Expectations of How the Internet/ICT Would Help the Firm

Firm Name	Manufacturer of	Main Expectations
Battery Solutions	Battery disposal services	Expand reach to large corporations and cities outside target market
Circle A Farms	Emu meat	Sell exotic meat in foreign markets
Comfortably Yours	Mastectomy bras	Expand into new markets due to limited competition, demand for this type of product
Consolidated Industries	Industrial soap	Provide better online customer service
Designed Outputs	ISO 9000 consulting	Develop online quality manuals
Euphonic Publishing	Original sheet music	Gain market share in large, closed market dominated by corporations
Genesis Apparel	Promotional products	Foster online communications strategy with customers
Great Lakes Rubber	Molded rubber products	Create an online customer service response center
Greenline Design	Architectural drawings	Download drawings
Midwest Bedding	Mattresses	Sell more mattresses to foreign markets
NetTechnology	Translation	Provide online translation instead of expensive express mailing of documents
Owosso Graphic Arts	High tech photoengraving	Educate customers and enhance online file transfer capabilities
Perich and Partners	Advertising	Create online marketing strategies for firms
Sebewaing Tools	Automotive supplier	Provide technical information and customer support
Stadium Club Foods	Award winning chili	Better compete with large food corporations

Source: McCue.

the firm's e-commerce strategy accordingly. The question that
dressed later is how to develop strategies to increase the num-
les based on the number of hits, *e.g.*, going from 1000:1 to

rse, most firms' hit/sale ratios in the studies were extremely
it is important that most enterprises in the study and in the
ice remain optimistic—and continue to learn—about how the
will help them because of the Internet's ability to enhance a
dibility, marketing, sales, and information sharing, integrating,
ig capacity.
, despite some disappointment in immediate sales, many firms
dy felt that the Internet provides substantially more advertising
ause it reaches a wider and more targeted market than tradi-
)motional media (i.e., firms can reach many more specific po-
ents). Reaching targeted customers in an inexpensive way was
t to the firms, and many firms therefore expressed willingness
promotional dollars in updating and expanding their site rather
nding funds on traditional promotional venues such as trade
ewspaper advertisements, etc. Firms that *did* have sales adopted
ve, multi-faceted approach to advertising their site. These firms
ie to communicate with potential clients in nontraditional
nternational markets due to *reactive* or *passive* promotion
search engines. They also had a *proactive* marketing approach
by the firm in which existing and potential customers were en-
to visit the site.

ns Learned: 1998

g are a few impressions the enterprises had after their first at-
) implement an e-commerce strategy:

he] Internet is good for sending an impression about my
iness, but it did not generate sales."
'Benefits of marketing on the Internet will be realized in
ee to five years; the sooner a business gets online, the
ner the business will notice a positive change in his or her
iness."
'I learned about the need to focus the content of my site in
ponse to my customers' need for information."
'Every morning I check our e-mail for requests from po-

due to too much competition on the Inter
culty luring existing and potential customer
found it difficult to register with search eng
intuitively obvious to customers who are
service on the Internet.

Overall, the greatest frustrations as these
products and services on the Internet were
the site, translating into a weak return on ir

For those firms in the United States,
US$1,500 to design a simple site and the av
maintenance fee. Research, prototype dev
updating, maintenance, and other costs can
e-commerce strategy to well over US$10,00(

Such significant cost of developing, desig
taining a site emphasizes the importance for
number of hits to the site (which is provided
number of total leads generated to the a
example, consider the experiences of these b
Exhibit 2.7.

Notice that there is no comparability of th
due to variability in sector competition, adve
nal factors such as customer service, capacity
a deal. A hit/sale ratio simply allows the firr
number of hits and the resultant sales are in

to adjus
will be a
ber of s
100:1.

Of cc
low, bu
marketp
Internet
firm's c
and sto!

In su
in the s'
value b
tional p
tential
importa
to inve.
than sp
shows,
a proac
were a
and/or
throug
initiate
courag

Less

Follow
tempt!

**EXHIBIT 2.7 Comparison of Total Visits,
August 1997–1998**

Firm Name	Type of Firm
Battery Solutions	Battery disposal firm
Comfortably Yours	Mastectomy bras
Euphonic Publishing	Original sheet music
Great Lakes Rubber	Molded rubber products
Greenline Design	Online drawings
Midwest Bedding	Mattresses
Sebewaing Tools	Automotive supplier

Source: McCue.

tential customers that visit our home page. Usually we have two or three e-mails. The good prospects are requests for our business services that we probably would not have received if we were not marketing on the Internet."

"Marketing on the Internet has made our business look more professional, places you with top people in your industry, helps you compete with large business, and helps broaden your customer base."

"We have developed a low cost high impact site which we feel will generate sales for us which would have been inaccessible without the development of our site."

"Right now, the Internet is everything it is meant to be but in total disarray. It is supposed to be the information super highway but for now it is like going onto the highway and once you are on it, you find out there is road construction everywhere and there isn't a map, and you don't know what to do, and then you realize that you are lost."

"Having a site adds tremendous value to a business—it contributes infinitely more than it costs. You have an international 'office' with little overhead. You can project an image that puts you in the enterprise league with the 'the big guys'."

"We would recommend that you consider utilizing this rather inexpensive marketing tool to improve your potential sales contacts as well as to maintain a high profile with your existing customers."

"The Internet is a wonderful research tool for anybody. It's a way to reach lots of potential customers. You can find information, products, and services easily. The trend to use the Internet for more ideas will grow and grow. The bad part is the spam e-mail that you receive. The frustrations are the pop-up sites that find their way to you unwanted. We have been very successful because of our Internet presence. Our site has been helpful for our customers and prospective clients. We intend in the future to be able to have our customers get reports over the 'Net concerning their orders that they have in our system."

This study revealed that frustrations with e-commerce remain, although technologies are maturing, and adjustments in strategies and models are being made. Some sites are becoming profitable. Yet most firms remain positive that e-commerce could benefit the business over time. Despite the bumpy ride and unmet sales expectations, most did not seek to abandon the Internet as an e-commerce strategy due to lack of sales. They viewed the Internet as a way to enhance services to customers, increase sales, and improve technological efficiencies in the firm.

They recognized, however, that an overall e-commerce strategy must be integrated throughout the firm, supported by a cross-cutting number of employees within the firm responsive to the clearly identified needs of targeted customers. The challenges of the new electronic marketplace may seem daunting, but they are doable, as you can see on many successful sites. This book will help you address these challenges for your firm.

3

Developing an E-Commerce Strategy

Developing a successful e-commerce strategy requires careful planning and commitment. E-commerce must be regarded as a long-term operation rather than a short-term profit-making opportunity. It must be an integral part of your overall business strategy.

Unfortunately, many e-commerce businesses do not consider e-commerce a serious business tool that requires planning, adoption, usage and monitoring. It involves technology, investment of time and money, and development of tactics about how to describe and target customers and how to respond to their online needs.

Developing a strategy has many benefits. First of all, it will confirm whether and when an Internet presence is desirable for your company. It will also enable you to make effective use of this powerful business tool. Another positive result is that, through the process of making your analyses and developing the strategy, you may identify areas in your operation that need refinement, adjustment, or internment, whether or not you decide to implement an e-commerce strategy.

Is Your E-Commerce Strategy Integrated into Your Business Strategy?

Think about this question for a moment. It should be obvious why your e-commerce strategy needs to be linked to the main objectives of the company. Yet, right now you may have one part of your team responsible for the company's overall marketing, expansion, and financing strategies while another team may be responsible for the overall technology, Internet, and systems strategies. Integrating these various

Exhibit 3.1 No Bid for eBay & Sothebys.com

It's been rumored for years, and now eBay and Sotheby's have finally joined hands. eBay will manage the online arm of the great but ailing auction house and try to do better than with its 1999 purchase of Butterfield & Butterfield (B&B). eBay apparently can't stop banging its head against the wall in fine art, antiques, and collectibles, and Sotheby's is desperate. Not ideal.

eBay's second try

The big recent news for eBay Round Two in the ring with the online fine art, antique, and big-ticket collectibles auction business is that the company will merge its eBay Premier site—a virtual ghost town—with Sothebys.com, the online presence of the venerable Sotheby's auction house. The new Sothebys.com site is to replace both its parents. eBay will manage the new site, and Sotheby's will use eBay's Live Auctions technology to enable online real-time auction bidding for some auctions in New York and London.

The 258-year-old Sotheby's and its arch-rival, the privately-held Christie's, have built large worldwide businesses, bringing together buyers and sellers and creating the premiere marketplaces for their luxury items. They are the Coke and Pepsi of their world, with titles changing hands back and forth. But publicly-traded Sotheby's has *not rewarded* its shareholders with the drink makers' returns. And both trusted auction house brand names have been tarnished recently by federal government antitrust investigations and settlements, as well as the conviction of former Sotheby's Chairman and still-majority shareholder A. Alfred Taubman for price-fixing with Christie's.

Rumors of an eBay-Sotheby's venture have swirled and been denied for years, but in 1999 the two chose sides. eBay bought distant number three auction house Butterfield & Butterfield, and Sotheby's allied online with Amazon to create sothebys.amazon.com. So why the new changes? Because the deals bombed, and the companies can't seem to stop making bad business decisions in this unique, idiosyncratic arena.

They've looked at art from both sides now

eBay wanted a piece of the higher-end art auction market when it snapped up distant number three auction house B&B in 1999 for US$260 million. Perhaps eBay failed to interest Sotheby's, Christie's, or up-and-comer Phillips, de Pury & Luxembourg, so it can hardly be faulted for buying an also-ran if the others had said "ix-nay" or proffered unreasonable terms. Bought in order to headline the eBay Premier business, B&B lacked the cache and the inventory of its bigger competitors and didn't grow into critical mass on eBay either. In July 2000, eBay laid off five percent of the B&B staff and curtailed vocal live B&B auctions. Not quite the return eBay got from buying half.com.

Today, the eBay Premier auction house page contains a bunch of linked houses, but paltry wares. Over half have nothing currently for sale, and the rest—except for

B&B and one other—link to another online flailing auction house aggregator. Despite links to other individuals and dealers from its home page, the eBay offering has never become a must-visit destination for the serious collector nor eBay's own huge customer base. Lose-lose. Premier has failed, and the new joint eBay-Sothebys.com site will replace it. eBay told members on its site that the deal "represents the next step in eBay's evolution of creating an online destination for high-end arts, antiques, and rare collectibles." More like, "Our next try to see if it works since it didn't the first time."

The flip side

Sotheby's has little choice, because the auction house giant is going South-by's. The economy's dive has reduced the market for luxury goods. The partnership with Amazon failed to help either party and ended in October 2000, after Amazon's reported expenditures of US$45 million. Sotheby's sports five years of flat to declining revenues, and had negative free cash flow of US$116 million for the nine months to September 2001. In fact, the company hasn't generated annual positive free cash flow since fiscal year 1998. Though Sotheby's breaks out only its Internet expenses and not revenues, management's comment in the 2000 10-K that it expected the operations to continue to be "dilutive to earnings" says it all.

Competitor Christie's has done well in response by publishing all its worldwide auction catalogs online and opening all live auctions to electronic bids from its site. Live bidding must still be in person or by phone, but you can place your opening bid and ceiling online, and the auctioneer bids it up (very much as you can do on eBay currently). Oddly, Sotheby's still acts as if the catalog business is a profit center, putting very few catalogs online and using Sothebys.com only for eBay-like, time-limited auctions.

Why it won't work

eBay and Sotheby's have different market constituencies, and both want what the other has. Good luck. Sotheby's thinks that eBay's 42 million registered users will flock to the Sotheby's brand for middle-to-low end purchases. Though they can't be truly compared, why would eBay users—admittedly more numerous but probably not more affluent—do what Amazon's did not?

eBay purportedly views Sotheby's as an entrée to bigger ticket and bigger fee income. It hasn't worked before, and even the addition of Sotheby's marquee name is unlikely to help now. Auction houses—online or offline—compete for sellers of high-priced art. It's an individualized, idiosyncratic business world where competition for sellers has reduced and often waived the seller's commission ("premium" in auction house parlance), based upon a number of individualized factors. Sellers also consider a dealer or auction house's abilities in such non-eBay niches as seller short-term financing, staff expertise (such as in authentication), and tax and insurance appraisal.

Worse, eBay's strength—its rating system and town square market approach—can only go so far to attract buyers and sellers of fine art when the system is

---

EXHIBIT 3.1 (Continued)

---

occasionally abused. In April 2001, three eBay sellers were charged with shill bidding to up the ante to over US$135,000 for a fake Richard Diebenkom painting. Two pled guilty and made restitution to buyers. This is not the kind of news that attracts conservative, high-end buyers and sellers. They know that Sotheby's will make them whole without a federal prosecution and before a seller's resources are gone.

In short, eBay's business model is, with limited exceptions, about scale and volume and time-limited auctions, with frenzied bidding at the last minute. The high-end international art market is about the world of the very rich, discretion, individual relationships, and auctions that extend for as many days as there are bids. Sothebys.com tries to fit a square peg in a round hole. Christie's has recognized that—but then, it has no pressure to serve public shareholders.

The dream of the joint venture is to marry Sotheby's trusted brand with eBay's customer base. eBay and Sotheby's may succeed in a niche market of lower-end fine art, antiques and collectibles, but this will at best add marginal revenues and profits to each. eBay's presumptive long-term hope that this may be a reverse slippery slope upwards to the larger ticket items will, I believe, be dashed, just as they were with Butterfield & Butterfield.

Source: Motley Fool, http://www.google.com/search?hl=en&q=No+Bid+for+ebay+and+sotheby&btnG=Google+Search.
©Copyright 1995–2005 The Motley Fool, Inc. (www.fool.com) All rights reserved.

---

activities into one overall plan appears obvious, yet many businesses even today are operating on two separate tracks: one for "traditional" business and others for the new Internet-based economy—and are not as successful as they had hoped to be.

The belief that a firm can transform itself into an "e-business" by simply establishing a site, and maybe adding hardware and installing software, is wrong and dangerous. Instead, to be successful in e-commerce, companies must incorporate e-business concepts and attitudes into their overall business strategies. Done well, an e-commerce initiative requires analyses and, more than likely, changes in strategy, orientation, organization, processes, and systems.

Indeed, in order to survive and thrive in today's global e-conomy, a company must at least:

- Recognize how e-commerce and ICT affect the entire enterprise.
- Define—or re-define—its marketing approach (e.g., how to expand into existing or new markets and know how to gain new customers).

- Identify ways in which technology will be employed in a strategic manner.

A good e-commerce and information and communications technology (ICT) strategy will improve the overall performance of your company as well as the efficiency and effectiveness of your employees. Also keep in mind that an e-commerce strategy and ICT system will not necessarily result in reduced numbers of employees but rather in smarter, more efficient, and more technologically savvy employees with redefined responsibilities. The following is a brief listing of the advantages of an e-commerce Web site.

Benefits of an E-Commerce Site

- An enhanced credibility by projecting a more solid, up-to-date professional image. *Not* being on the Web with a good, updated and transactional site will make customers wonder about your business.
- An additional vehicle to promote products and services. You now have a way to reinforce your message from other media.
- Promotion in more markets at no additional expense. Your extended reach provides market access you could not anticipate because customers can now find you so much more easily.
- Easy answering of questions on products or services. Automating the answers to frequently-asked questions (FAQs) will save staff time and therefore, money. And you will be providing consistent answers that are always accurate. But don't forget the importance of allowing the customer to *talk* with someone.
- Online quotations. Allowing online quotation allows for a simpler and more streamlined method to communicate with potential buyers.
- Improved response time to customer queries. Although nothing can beat the power of a phone to phone call, allowing customers to contact you via e-mail or online video conference will increase your customer service quality and efficiency.
- Quicker and easier feedback from customers. This, too, can be automated, with a click-on "contact us" feature. Their queries and concerns can then be assembled, analyzed and mined for potential improvements in products and services.

- Improved customer service. Responding quickly to customer needs make customers happy. So many businesses do not embrace this simple fact.
- Same-day service or service beyond regular working hours. You can provide service without being locked into a particular place and time.
- Marketing by e-mail. Lists targeted to specific clients can easily be set up for fast broadcasting to segmented constituencies. (See the section on e-mails in Chapter 5, the Secrets of Electronic Commerce.)
- Paperless documentation. Records are stored instantly on computers.

Benefits of an E-Commerce Strategy: A Before and After Comparison

The side-by-side comparison in Exhibit 3.2 shows where technology can help you with information consolidation, advertising, product catalogs, purchase orders and requisitioning, approval, inventory and shipping and receiving, billing and payment, routing and customer service, and tracking.

Common Mistakes Firms Make in Building an E-Commerce Strategy

Since the Web began, many e-commerce sites have come and gone, come and changed, come and remained stagnant. What went right? What went wrong? Here are some errors in thoughts and actions which too many firms make:

- Believing that having a site will automatically lead to instant sales.
- Believing that using the Internet is an easy way to make one's business and products known worldwide. There are about a third of a trillion pages visible on the World Wide Web and the number is growing exponentially. Being present on the Web does not mean being visible.
- Believing that an Internet site will replace other promotional strategies rather than fit into the firm's overall promotional strategy.

EXHIBIT 3.2 Key Business Function Before "E" and After "E"

	Before	After
Information Consolidation	Staff "hoarded" information	MIS centralizes information for all to see
Advertising	Offline, mass market, expensive	MIS centralizes information for all to see
Product Catalogs	Paper-based, storage and distribution problems	Online, multiple photos possible, less expensive
Purchase Orders and Requisitioning	Sent via mail or fax, difficult for the customer to determine actual costs	Online software helps the customer determine costs before ordering, and allow easier submission and receipt of purchase orders
Approval	Difficult to prove final approval authority given in person, via fax, etc.	Online approval allows for system integration, more coordinated processing, and ease of tracking approval process for accountability
Inventory, and Shipping and Receiving	Paper-based, not coordinated with other software-based programs within the company to offer "Just in Time" delivery	Online inventory systems allow customer to order directly from the site, and easier coordination among departments to more quickly fill customer orders
Billing and Payment	Nonautomated systems are costly and result in human errors	Online billing systems are coordinated, automatic, and less expensive.
Routing and Customer Service	Telephone-based customer service, not usually coordinated within the company, customer service agent very important to answer customer query	Internet-based customer service, coordinated, but often not as satisfying to the customer because of delay in response, and automated online responses which do not answer specific customer questions
Tracking	Customers were often unable to track the details regarding shipment of their order	Online tracking systems significantly reduce customer queries

- Not spending enough time to plan and organize the site's content architecture/navigation/layout to make it easy for the customer to use the site. The fastest way to lose potential customers is to make the site too difficult or too time-consuming or too frustrating to use.
- Insufficient testing of the site to make sure it works the way it should for visitors to the site.
- Designing a site that makes it difficult for customers to identify advantages of the product or quickly understand why they should buy from you.
- Not updating the site frequently.
- Not responding within three days or (preferably) less to e-mailed customer requests for information.
- Believing that middlemen or intermediaries will automatically disappear with the advent of the Internet. Many manufacturers are not equipped and/or are not willing to deal with the individual firm or person ordering a product.
- Believing that the Internet will level the playing field between large and small enterprises. As in traditional business, established brand names and adequate financial resources continue to be the predominate factors for success on the Internet.

Traps to Avoid When Developing an E-Commerce Strategy

Not Seeking Advice. Firms that are new to e-commerce often fail to perform a very simple exercise, resulting in a site that is unresponsive to the needs of the customer. Many do not ask their customers what they need from an online presence, nor do they ask the technical questions necessary to determine how internal and external systems will integrate.

Not Obtaining Management Commitment. Ensure that top management is committed to the development of the strategy. Though one person should be assigned the overall responsibility of ensuring the development and the implementation of the strategy, the company's functional divisions—management, administration, finance, marketing, production, training—should be involved in its formulation.

Not Keeping Management in Control. Senior management of businesses tends to give up control of their e-commerce strategy. What often happens is that young, energetic, technically savvy, and well-intentioned lower management employees with no strategic, marketing, or financial management experience soon clash with upper management. As a result, everyone becomes frustrated with the lack of performance, and remain confounded, confused, or not willing to invest the time needed to fully understand this phenomenon.

Not Conducting Solid Market Research. Market research, online and offline, enables the strategist to study target market demographics, political, and socioeconomic conditions; study online activities by industry, country, and product; identify e-commerce marketing techniques; conduct surveys, hold focus groups on particular topics, including the technical aspects of what is and what is not possible/probable/ preferable.

Not Analyzing Market Research. Analyze your research to confirm whether or not the product is suitable for sale on the Internet and whether or not it will sell in certain markets; whether your product design, size, color and other characteristics will be attractive to specific markets; whether it will meet the preferences of people who seek to buy online; whether your plans are appropriate for the users' needs.

Not Acknowledging How Buyers Make Decisions. Address how buyers make purchasing decisions on the Internet. The most important factor in a buyer's decision to purchase, online or offline, is whether or not he or she trusts the seller. Every effort should therefore be made to ensure that your site projects your trustworthiness. Other determining factors include the length of time spent online, the technical abilities of the person online (which are greatly increasing as e-commerce becomes an entrenched sales mechanism), familiarity with the product, and the shopper's need to save time or money, along with the product itself and the performance of the vendor.

Lack of Overall Marketing Communications. Firms often fail to sell as much as they expected to sell online because they are unaware of the low-cost, or no-cost, marketing opportunities available to them. In addition to the usual online marketing techniques, the best offline marketing opportunities are still provided by catalogs, international buyer programs, agent/distributor services, publicity and advertising, catalog exhibitions, and trade shows.

Not Diversifying the Firm's Methods of Operations. Many firms use direct e-commerce as their only means of distribution. A site gives the enterprise maximum control over marketing, financing, and market growth. However, other methods of advertising, promotion, and distribution still exist. They include appointment of a commissioned e-commerce sales agent, letting an e-commerce management company handle sales, appointing an online sales representative, negotiating a distribution agreement, a licensing joint venture, and offshore production. In addition to helping exporters to implement successful e-commerce strategies, these methods will enable them to benefit from the know-how and contacts of a partner experienced in e-commerce.

Not Determining the Optimum E-commerce Price. Many online retailers and suppliers find it difficult to price their products and services for online sales. The following are various specific costs that contribute to the determination of the overall unit price of a product. They should be addressed in financial projections and in a three-year budget:

- Web site design
- Hardware and software
- Site updating
- Site monitoring for messages
- Web order processing
- Electronic marketing
- Percentage mark-up
- Sales commissions
- Freight forwarding fees
- Financing costs
- Letter-of-credit or other payment processing fee
- Freight charges
- Unloading at terminals
- Insurance
- Translation(s)
- Credit terms
- Payment schedules
- Payment currencies
- Warehousing costs
- After-sales servicing
- Cost of replacing damaged goods

Getting Your Strategy Started:
Where Is the Company Heading?

Before fully committing to an e-commerce initiative, first consider where your company plans or should be planning to move strategically in the next few years. The Basic E-Commerce Strategic Plan (outlined at the end of the chapter) will help you identify the following:

- The core competency and focus of the company over the next few years. What makes your company unique and how can you remain ahead of the competition?
- Existing and new markets and expectations for growth. Why are you selecting new target markets or why are you focusing on existing ones?
- Expectations of how your products and services will change during that time. What new innovations in marketing, customer service, and product design must you compete with, or have you planned?
- Key ways in which your products and services will be different from competitors. Is your strategy based on features/benefits, price, quality, reliable delivery schedules, new technology, and/or being able to customize the product to your client's needs?
- Critical changes in customer support, conformity to international standards, or greater quality. How will you delight your customer with an improved product or service?
- How e-commerce may affect your traditional supply chain in terms of purchasing, inventory management, customer management and logistics. What are the changes that will be needed in your policies, processes, systems, and procedures?
- Prioritization of goals, risks to the company, and change management issues. Some staff members may be resistant to change. How will you articulate your goals and plan for smooth implementation of them?
- Staff, financial and technical resources needed, the project plan, timelines, and financial budgets. In other words, who, what, when, and how much is needed to achieve your strategic goals?

Preparing a strategy for your company will allow you to understand the types of e-commerce systems, the benefits and risks of online selling and buying, and the various options you can select so that you can successfully implement online buying and selling systems.

By being aware of the latest developments in e-commerce and ICT systems, processes, and procedures, you will be better prepared to make informed decisions as you implement the strategy. After all, successful e-commerce is simply a matter of first identifying your strategy, allocating scarce resources, and then understanding and using the appropriate technology available to you.

An e-commerce strategy does not differ fundamentally from any other business plan. However, before you draw your strategy, you must ensure that your company understands the characteristics of the online marketplace compared to the traditional. In the online marketplace, these different characteristics include the:

- Global nature of the competition.
- Global nature of reactions to your site.
- Technical and regulatory requirements for online sales.
- Role that information plays in electronic trade.

Four Strategic Options for E-Commerce

Here are four strategic options you want to consider when establishing an e-commerce strategy: targeted customer and/or supplier relationship, transactional/automated e-commerce, participation in e-marketplaces, and a mostly informational, open-to-all Web site. Keep in mind that these are not either-or options. They are not mutually exclusive. Indeed, you can employ one or more or all on your site. You might want to start out with one option and then expand to the others as e-commerce grows as part of your business strategy. These options should, however, be considered individually, because each has its own unique advantages and approaches.

Targeted Customer and/or Supplier Relationship

If you have established a preferred customer and/or supplier relationship with one or several primary companies and enjoy trust and a solid relationship with them, you will want your site to reflect that you understand and respond to their specific needs and requirements.

The benefits of this type of option include the:

- Ability to customize products for preferred customers.
- Increased efficiency of order transactions.
- Ability to serve your customer's needs quickly.
- Ability to create similar relationships with other buyers by creating shared interfaces and connectivity with other buyers.

It is critical to gain your clients' input to implement this type of e-commerce strategy successfully. Without your customers' and/or suppliers' input, your site software will be virtually useless. It is amazing how many firms do not obtain such input. However, a customer-centric system may entail high up-front costs: each customer may have differing data standards, requiring multiple interfaces, and the software available for e-commerce may lack compatibility. Yet these obstacles can easily be overcome by cooperatively working together to build interfaces between your respective systems so that in the longer run, your up-front investment will pay off.

Transactional/Automated E-Commerce

Setting up a transactional site allows customers to buy from you online (sales), track the order status of orders being shipped (logistics), and submit questions and requests for quotations online (customer service).

The benefits of establishing such a site include:

- Direct entry of order information by the customer to database.
- Reducing possibility of error, improving customer service.
- Minimizing fulfillment time.
- Increasing production efficiency.
- Establishing new ways to provide customer service, thus attracting new customers.

Automated e-commerce sites create a continuous, uninterrupted supply-chain process by integrating buyers and sellers into one electronic chain through seamless, electronically initiated and electronically monitored exchanges of information. Automated systems range from the planning and forecasting of the buyer to the delivery and payment of the seller, regardless of the product or service. They represent the highest degree of electronic integration among buyers and suppliers, facilitating the development of the supply chain over the Internet into a continuous, uninterrupted electronic process. An automated system requires maximum standardization and integration of your firm's operations. By using such a system, you will create efficiencies because information is entered only once—and accurately—to trigger an automatic supply chain operation between buyer and supplier.

However, these systems can require significant up-front investment. In addition to installing software, hardware, and ERP systems, other expenses include catalogs and content development, supplier/buyer negotiations, training clients and employees, licensing fees, maintenance, and buyer/seller systems integration. Keep in mind it is possible to avoid some of these costs by purchasing e-commerce services through ASPs, those firms that provide outsourcing of financial database management and run software and e-commerce applications.

A limitation of this e-commerce strategy is an overall lack of standards and lack of compatible software. Currently, firms can exchange data if each uses the same electronic data exchange format (e.g., EDI or XML) or if either partner develops interfaces to translate the other partner's data into a compatible format. An alternative is to purchase a large and costly e-commerce software system able to interface with other e-commerce systems.

In the future, intercompatible e-commerce software packages will be developed and marketed to a widespread user group similar to how Microsoft's intercompatible PC software packages took hold among most of the world's PC users. Also, XML standards will make it easier to transfer data without a pre-harmonized data format.

Participation in E-Marketplaces

An Internet marketplace is a site on the Internet where sellers and buyers can post offers, communicate their interest in these offers, and finalize the business transaction without verbally talking or exchanging paper documents.

Marketplaces are created to find a larger range of suppliers/buyers to obtain better prices and to earn money by charging for each transaction that takes place in the marketplace.

Marketplaces can be general or industry-specific and can be only for buying or selling or be more fully integrated with holistic services including credit reporting, shipment monitoring, legal advisement, online training, and virtual conferences.

Your decision to participate in a marketplace or not depends on several factors such as the number, type, size, and location of your customers.

The benefits of e-marketplaces include:

- Gaining daily access to global market information such as current selling prices in various regions.
- Tracking sales activities of competitors.
- Identifying early trends in your industry.

However, the risks of participating in marketplaces often include data exchange security risks, potential exposure of final sale price (known as bid acceptance) to competitors, and current lack of standards among various marketplaces regarding industry lingo and user interfaces. As a result, there are steep learning curves in individual marketplaces but these are expected to be corrected by market shakeout leading to more efficient and uniform marketplaces.

Mostly Informational, Open-to-All Web Site

The vast majority of "e-commerce" Web sites are simply informational, not transactional. They are open to all who visit the Web site. Because most sites are not fully transactional, of the estimated 265 million business-oriented sites posted on the Internet as of 2002, 85 percent of them are mostly informational, open to all.

Many high-tech, highly-complex or highly-misunderstood businesses employ these kinds of sites to disseminate information about the company to prevent misunderstandings or the misuse of products and/or services. Others use the information only strategy to provide automated customer service, provide technical information about a product or service, or simply to convey quick information to those who do not know anything about the company, thus reducing the cost of advocacy and marketing.

Goals of Your E-Commerce Strategy

As you begin to develop your strategy and implement its related activities, first articulate your main—even subsidiary—goals for your company. Remember to include at least these three main goals:

- Find new clients for your company.
- Maintain and respond to your current and future clients and their needs.
- Improve your profitability through use of technology.

To reach these goals, businesses developing e-commerce strategies should be concerned with four basic, essential elements:

- Increasing customers by attracting them to the Web site.
- Developing a site that responds to a customer's need for information.
- Creating the ability to place orders safely online.
- Designing a site that is graphically and technologically able to achieve these goals.

By the time you have implemented your strategy and gone online, your firm should also have:

- Technical and supply capacity for selling products and services on a global online market.
- Production and sales processes and trained personnel in place that will enable the firm to handle a significant increase in business from current and new customer locations.

Differences between Traditional and Online Sales

In getting started, first understand that there are differences between the "traditional" ways of selling and otherwise doing business and how e-commerce and ICT has changed things. There are clear distinctions between traditional and online sales that should be taken into account while developing the right e-commerce strategy (see Exhibit 3.3).

The Importance of Communicating Changes to Staff

As you begin and progress with your e-commerce strategy, a fundamental issue is ensuring the input, support, and agreement of all the people in the company, from key decision-makers and thought leaders to line and support staff who will be using new technologies and marketing approaches.

Input from all sources should be considered and your strategic decisions must be clearly communicated in order to avoid confusion and uncertainties. Many times, unfortunately, senior management will devise and implement an e-commerce strategy in consultation with Web designers and a few key staff members, leaving others to wonder how "going e" will affect them.

Without this information, employees will remain outside the change loop. Staff may say that they accept the new e-commerce initiative, but then refuse to use new technology.

Many employees are resistant to change because they fear losing control, do not understand the change, or simply are too comfortable with the way things were done in the past. They, in turn, may influence other staff members with negative and critical comments. This negative thinking often occurs because often employees may be concerned that

Exhibit 3.3 Traditional Sales and Online Sales: The Differences

Traditional	Online
Initial contacts to customers are through cold calling, fairs, personal contacts.	Initial contacts are through e-marketplaces, online searching, and e-mail marketing.
Customers obtained by your being at the right place at the right time.	Customer must visit the site.
Uncertainty ends when the buying process begins.	Uncertainty starts when the buying process begins.
Buyer's importance on transaction focused on the product; buying processes are not automated (possibility of errors).	Buyer's importance on transaction focused on the buying process; using technology will reduce human error since most processes will be automated.
Promotional material comprised of brochures, faxes, ads, publicity, and mass or targeted mailing.	Promotional material comprised of online publications, e-mail messages, and linking combined with traditional marketing.
Establishment of an offer through mailing, faxes, etc.	Establishment of an offer through e-mail.
Delivery of goods through mailing, transportation systems.	Delivery of goods through mailing, transportation systems, downloading.
Buying process has minimum initial learning costs.	Buying process has high initial learning and technological costs.
Payment through mailing of the bill.	Payment through mailing of the bill or via the Internet.
Useful for products of high complexity and/or little standardization.	Useful for products of little complexity and/or high standardization.

Source: McCue.

new technology, systems, organization charts, and redefined responsibilities will take their jobs away or lessen the influence of their jobs due to increased efficiencies from technology.

Therefore, your requests for information and your management decisions should be conveyed in an open manner to allow staff to have an opportunity to contribute ideas and the time to adjust to possible changes. This will also serve to illustrate how responsibilities and duties may change. Sharing your e-commerce strategy with all staff and communicating how the new strategy will change the traditional ways of doing business for the better is vitally important to the success of your strategy. It will be well worthwhile to motivate and train employees, encourage them. Also, you should not back down when—if—you face resistance.

Often employees will perceive e-commerce as a threat either because they are afraid of being replaced or they will have to learn new duties. The message is that technology and new processes will not really replace your people, if they can and wish to be re-trained. Your people will be more efficient, effective, increase their skills, and increase and diversify their responsibilities. An entire chapter could be written on how traditional employee roles will change as a result of e-commerce and ICT, but the larger point is that most people will have their jobs redefined (see Changes in Organizational Structure in Chapter 6, Trends). With training, they will perform very well.

Reassure the staff that it will remain an integral part of your team. As examples:

- Management information system personnel will integrate employees' separate databases into one integrated system.
- Marketing managers will make "cold calls" using instant messaging, e-mail, and videoconferencing.
- Marketing executives will prepare e-mailing lists and marketing campaigns using e-mail and the Internet.
- Communication officers will prepare newsletters and magazines mostly for reading on the Internet.
- Accountants will integrate their databases into the entire company and those of customers.

This new approach will be foreign to many inside the company as well as for customers who may prefer the "old way" of doing business with your firm.

E-Market Factor Assessment

Because the Internet is available to people all over the world, your site may attract potential buyers from other countries. Market research will help you to determine which foreign markets have the best potential for your products and services to be sold online. You should select a few target markets on the basis of such factors as the Internet infrastructure; demographic, physical, political, economic, social and cultural environments; market accessibility; and the opportunities they offer for your products.

Conducting a thorough e-market factor assessment will help you to estimate demand for your product or services and to assess how well your firm will perform in specific markets. Although Internet sites will have a great deal of the information you seek, your federal government—and many state and provincial governments—more than likely has an export assistance program that you could tap into.

In order to arrive at a final selection of two to three foreign markets that you could target using online marketing, customer service and payment options, you should assess up to 10 countries that appear to offer import opportunities for your product.

To carry out an e-market factor assessment, you should ask at least the following questions regarding several aspects of foreign markets:

Population:
- What is the overall population of the country and its growth and density trends?
- Is the population of targeted age groups adequate (e.g., 1–10, 11–24, 25–40, 41–60, etc.)?
- How is the population distributed between the urban, suburban, and rural areas?
- What percentage of the population is defined as middle class? What is the per capita income? Have income levels increased over time?
- What are the levels of disposable income?
- What are the expenditure patterns?
- What percentage of the population is literate? What is the average educational level achieved?
- What percentage of the population speaks your targeted business languages?

Infrastructure and logistics:
- Is the Internet available in urban, suburban, and rural areas?
- If so, what percentage of the population has access to the Internet in their offices and homes?
- What are the shipping distances from your point of export to the point of entry and final destination in the country?

- Are there adequate shipping, packaging, unloading, and other local distribution networks?
- What is the average age and quality of the transportation and telecommunication infrastructure?
- Is online customer service acceptable to customers in the target market or will customer care be provided by telephone, e-mail, or fax?

Governmental and legal environment:
- Is the system of government conducive to conducting business there?
- To what degree is the government involved in private business transactions?
- What is the government's attitude to importing?
- Is the political system stable or do governing coalitions change frequently?
- Does the government seek to dismantle quotas, tariffs, and other trade barriers?
- Is the country committed to fostering higher levels of foreign trade?
- Is the market closed to foreigners, despite a free and open appearance?
- What are the documentary requirements and import regulations affecting the product or service you sell?
- What intellectual property protection laws will apply to your product?
- Does the judicial system offer a fair and unbiased review of commercial disputes arising from online transactions?
- Are tax laws fair to online sellers? What is the rate of tax on repatriated profits?
- What legal aspects affect distribution agreements in the country?

Economic factors:
- What is the county's gross national product and its balance of payments?
- What is the percentage share of imports and exports in the overall economy?
- What is the country's import-to-export ratio?
- What is the country's inflation rate?
- What are its currency or exchange regulations?

Social and cultural similarities/differences relative to home market:
- What religious beliefs, if any, have an impact upon the acceptance or use of the product?
- What are the attitudes towards foreign products?
- What are the social courtesies (i.e., introductions, greetings, use of business cards, entering and leaving home and/or places of business) of which you need to be aware?
- What are some business practices of your current or potential clients that may be different from yours, including hours of business?
- Are there colors, specific flowers, or gifts that may unintentionally offend?

Product/service:
- Is the product or service understood and accepted by the country?
- Will the product or service need translation or adaptation?
- Is there an identified need to purchase your product or service online in the country?
- What percentage of the product is or will be produced in the country and what percentage is imported?
- Are there climatic and weather variations that may affect your product or service?
- How many foreign and domestic competitors are in the country now? From which regions?

After carrying out research on several countries to obtain answers to the questions listed above—and any more that are appropriate to your situation—rate each country according to an e-market condition scale of 1 (poor) to 5 (excellent). Enter the points in a table similar to the one in Exhibit 3.4. Sum up the points. The higher the score, the greater the likelihood that the country concerned will offer a suitable market to sell your products and services online.

Strategic Networking: Enlightened Networking with People, Organizations

Although it may appear unusual to include networking in a chapter on strategy, the decision to network or not is one that should be raised at this point, not after all other issues have been considered and decided and systems are in place. Networking here is not meant to be networking

Exhibit 3.4 E-Market Factor Assessment Table

Market Factor	Country A	Country B	Country C
Demographic/Physical Environment			
Population: size, growth, density trend			
Age distribution			
Population distribution			
Per capita income: current status, distribution, and potential for growth			
Income distribution			
Disposable income levels			
Literacy and educational levels			
Languages, including English			
Infrastructure and logistics			
Availability of Internet, where			
Percentage with access to Internet			
Shipping distance and frequency			
Freight facilities			
Regional and local distribution systems			
Internet and telecommunication network			
Possibility for online customer service			
Political Environment			
System of government			
Government involvement in business			
Attitudes to foreign trade			
Political stability and continuity			
Fair and free trade mindset			
National trade development priorities			
Documentary requirements			
Intellectual property protection			
Judicial system			
Tax laws and policies			
Distribution agreements			
Economic Environment			
Overall level of development			
Economic growth: GNP, balance of payments			
Import to export ratio			
Inflation rate			
Currency and foreign exchange regulations			

(Continued)

EXHIBIT 3.4 (Continued)

Market Factor	Country *A*	Country *B*	Country *C*
Social and Cultural Environment			
Religious beliefs			
Language barriers			
Social courtesies			
Similarities/differences relative to home market			
Cultural practices			
Product Potential			
Product acceptance			
Product adaption			
Online purchase potential			
Customer needs			
Domestic production, imports, consumption			
Climatic and weather variation			
Exposure to, and acceptance of, product			
Competition			

Source: McCue.

as in computer systems hookups, but in contacts with people, companies, industries, governments and similar groups for specific reasons. Discussed below are several aspects for such consideration.

Why Networking Is Important

Niches, efficiencies, and growth within the firm, the sector, and country occur when these strategic networks share knowledge and use modern business e-models and technology to create vertical and horizontal networks. This will contribute to the flourishing of the Internet and e-commerce for all, rather than continue to the detriment of the current duplication, unnecessary incompatibility and variations in quality and standards.

In the public sector, for example, an integrated Export Assistance Network at the national level can be developed by having organizations offer more specialized services, rather than offering all services to all people. Such a network (online or onsite) could be developed to offer truly one-stop assistance with specialization, thus forcing the variety of kindred organizations to identify their specific service delivery niche. Such a network carves niches, reduces competition for funding and clients, reduces duplication and overlap of service provision, improves community development and local interaction, and provides a coordinated approach to national service delivery among disparate organizations. As another example, in the United States, Small Business Development Centers have not developed enough specialization and niches.

In the private sector, businesses within a sector that share a strategic vision can create greater efficiencies and standards in electronic commerce. For example, all professionals within the plastics industry could create a strategic horizontal network to understand, develop, and thrive in an electronic marketplace better.

To improve strategic networking, communication and co-operation, individuals must build better networks . . . or go from "us versus them" . . . or go from "me to we." *How* this can be achieved in the context of communication, cooperation, standardization, best practices, professional development, and improved use of online service delivery mechanisms is discussed below.

Results: Improved Communication and Cooperation

Improved Relationships among National and Local Networks. Often international or national networks are administered through a rigid hierarchical structure. Dissemination of funding and information and dictating of goals is "top-to-bottom," from the international to national to local networks. Typically, individuals in the local network view the national administrative organization as an intrusive, out-of-touch regulator, not a strategic partner with vision to create programs and services to jointly develop software, offer training programs for employees, or create online trading communities. What usually occurs is that individuals separately develop technology, software, programs, services, and products in a vacuum. This results in an unclear, frustrated, competitive, unproductive strategic relationship.

Often communication and collaboration are viewed as uncompetitive, collusionary, and placing profit and new discoveries at risk. However, it is necessary in this competitive global economy that national organizations and private sector groups adapt ways to improve communication and strategic orientation in ways listed below:

Offer Vertical and Horizontal Discussion Groups. The importance of communication between professionals within a network and among networks to share information, debate, collaborate, develop ideas, etc., cannot be underestimated. Professionals within a sector, especially in sectors where e-commerce and ICT is so misunderstood, should be able to share views, best practices, and answer questions on a more regular basis than once a year at a national meeting or in sector-specific magazines, if at all.

Via online discussion forums, these networked professionals can inexpensively and efficiently post ideas, solicit answers/reactions, and share knowledge on particular areas of interest to the professional, and provide direct assistance to a colleague in need of assistance (e.g., e-commerce, international trade, legal issues, partnerships, training modules, strategic planning, etc.). Certainly communication and collaboration with individuals formerly viewed as competitors will be seen as unusual. However, online discussions are a productive way to increase efficiencies, learn new skills, coalesce, and collaborate with a network of like-minded professionals.

Create an E-Mail Newsletter and/or Online Magazine. Creating an e-mail newsletter that is sent to all professionals within a strategic network will help identify best practices and give kindred professionals "need-to-know-to-grow" information regarding e-commerce and ICT.

Create National Training Institutes by Sector. Establishing online professional development training for the network gives individuals in enterprises within a particular industry sector a comparable, current, and equal knowledge base. It may be untraditional thinking for networks to assume responsibility for training and education. Yet e-commerce and technologies change so quickly within an industry, it is impossible for universities to provide a core basis of education on such highly variable, changing, and specific issues within a sector. If e-commerce is to flourish within industries, consistent and wide-spread training developed by the private sector is critically important.

Develop a List of Best Practices. Look at competitive and comparable sites and learn what they do best. Tailor what they do to what you could and should do. Create new practices. (See Exhibit 3.5.)

Create an Online Database of Network Talent. Often enterprises are unable to find the specific answer to a technical question because local expertise on a particular subject is not readily available. Therefore, a network of professionals and their specific skills be identified in a database. For example, refer to the Service Corps of Retired Executives national network databank of 605 business-related skills (http://www.score.org/onlinebin/skills/). This online database is a source of expertise no matter

---

EXHIBIT 3.5 Examples of Potential Best Practices

Offer Network-Developed and Distributed Products and Services. Most national networks do not offer consistent, well-designed, quality products and services throughout their delivery system. Businesses are not using standard software and communication and information technology, resulting in incompatibility and frustration among businesses seeking to integrate their business systems.

Focus on Star Performers. Identifying "star performers" or "islands of excellence" will allow others within the network to emulate innovations. For instance, the boat building industry could conduct a survey to identify unique, innovative, and cost-effective ways of using the Internet and ICT to improve customer service, develop Internet-based distance learning education, evaluate new approaches within the industry, foster e-commerce strategies, and learn from each other, etc. They are doing this now by spying on each other's sites, monitoring how technology and marketplaces are being used, and how customers are cared for. But there is no organized, collaborative mechanism established that would help leapfrog the industry into making e-commerce a sales, marketing, and communication force.

Develop an Innovation Fund. Industries should offer an "innovation fund" so firms could benefit from and disseminate excellent new software systems, business models, products, programs and services that are being independently developed. This would encourage and reward professionals who have developed innovative e-commerce products and other successful mechanisms to deliver inventive and quality e-commerce products, programs, and services.

Create an Advisory Council. Strategic vertical and horizontal networks should create a special, limited-term Advisory Council to determine an overall national and sector-specific electronic commerce strategy for enteprises. The council could identify specific products and programs to be developed in partnership with network members. This assumes that there is a national focal point or co-ordinating mechanism to develop a national e-commerce strategy and that firms within an industry are willing to work together.

Provide In-Depth Counselor Training. One reason e-commerce consultants often provide such low-level assistance or basic information is the lack of advanced training or knowledge advancement. A few of the critical areas in which anyone involved with e-commerce must be well trained are:

- site design for marketing and systems integration,
- automated e-procurement systems,
- communications and networking,
- online marketing and marketing research,

- Web-based information architecture,
- finance and financial accounting,
- electronic payment systems,
- computer security,
- e-commerce systems design,
- supply chain management,

- e-commerce law and regulation,
- pricing,
- information systems development,
- order fulfillment,
- multimedia,
- databases,

- electronic negotiation,
- intelligent agents,
- online customer service and help facilities, and
- mobile e-commerce.

Source: McCue.

what the location of the enterprise, thus improving the depth of counseling and access to expertise.

Determine Enterprise Needs. An annual assessment to identify specific informational and technical assistance needs of buyers and suppliers in an industry should be undertaken by the network. Specific online systems, software, and integration tools, and professional development training could then be developed in direct response to these needs.

Develop Online Answer Desks. There is a need for better use of online communication and information dissemination technology so that more within the network can understand electronic commerce. In light of efficient and effective 21st century technology, we must dispense with the idea that counseling and training must be done in person. Therefore, networks are strongly encouraged to develop online, e-mail-based "Answer Desks" and answers to frequently asked questions based on the speciality of experts, regardless of geographical location. If there is no concerted effort to respond to the needs for electronic commerce, the community of enterprises in a country will be rendered uncompetitive, unresponsive, and behind the times in terms of using electronic commerce and related technologies.

Coalescing to Use Technology to Reshape E-Commerce Sectors

As businesses develop their e-commerce strategies, networking among kindred groups of individuals working within a sector is imperative, even though individuals in private sector firms are not accustomed to partner with competitors. Plastics researchers, cell phone manufacturers, manufacturers of automotive components, banana growers, database software designers, online grocery stores, and universities are just a few of thousands of profit-oriented organizations that compete with each other online and offline by seeking the same clients and offering similar products and services. Yet with the advent of the Internet and increasingly sophisticated technologies, it is important to coalesce and communicate to create a unified industry with common standards, platforms, business models, etc. This idea may be antithetical to traditional ways of competing in the business world, but more businesses will survive and thrive with increased cooperation, reduced duplication, and collaboration.

Many systems will require standardized and accepted systems, policies, processes, procedures, and global standards if online marketplace commerce is to flourish within the individual firms and the industry. The trading of unprocessed citrus fruits, for example, is constantly changing in terms of online auctioning techniques, order fulfilment, financing, payment, customer service, portals, and other systems. Standardized and accepted systems, policies, processes, procedures, and accepted global standards must be developed and incorporated within an industry if online commerce is to flourish within the industry. Now growers, banks, systems designers, portal developers, shippers, and buyers do not share information, collaborate, communicate, and network regarding how to create a seamless online citrus fruit industry. The problems are exacerbated with incompatible and competing software, multiple competing and confusing auctions, non-standard payment systems, and not integrated, out-of-date information. The struggles go on.

And certainly struggling for standardization is not unique to the citrus fruit industry. The same is happening in the telecommunication industry in Switzerland as Swisscom remains dominant over smaller firms that are not collaborating as to how to redefine the industry in light of the new electronic marketplace and technologies. As a result, Swisscom still dominates.

Billions of dollars were lost in the dot.com implosion in April of 2001 because individual firms attempted to create business models within a sector by testing new market techniques, using incompatible software, and refusing to network and communicate among industry professionals. Everyone was looking out for themselves to create their own models, standards, systems, and ways of creating empires within industries. And individuals within the industry are still attempting to dominate.

Yet most sectors still struggle to develop viable business models. With firms "going it alone," the results are inconsistency, incompatibility, and too much independence. Moreover, their efforts are dominated by large corporations who are defining the new marketplaces, not because they are better, but because they are bigger.

We realize that competition is the foundation of any sector and competition will dominate once again as soon as marketplaces, software, norms, and systems have become standardized within electronic commerce sectors and marketplaces. However, until this happens, communication, collaboration, and "enlightened networking" are imperative within industries. Enlightened networking discourages information hoarding, independence, individualism, and an "us versus them" mentality within an industry. In the 21st century, enlightened networking in uncertain and weak marketplaces demands a "standardized industry" with accepted ways of using industry-wide technologies, systems, policies, processes, and procedures.

Now more than ever, strategic vertical and horizontal networking is imperative if e-commerce is going to evolve as a significant marketing, communication, sales, service, shipping, and financing medium. Today thousands of industries and millions of firms around the globe are trying to define e-commerce standards, find ways to collaborate with the competition to create common systems and interfaces, encourage customers to "go e," and expand their customer base using the Internet and technology.

Once standardization is achieved, businesses within the sector will be able to offer any-time, any-place services, information, and products to give customers what they need and when they need it.

Right now, most customers within an online sector are confused, frustrated, and have not maximized the extent to which they can be integrated into an online marketplace to find information, receive targeted messages of interest to them, share common databases, and quickly place, receive, and pay for their orders, etc. As a consequence, there are confused customers and weak markets that should be thriving in an e-commerce setting.

Strategic Vertical Networking

A strategic vertical network can be described as a "formal, top-down" network from the international to national to state to regional to local levels. A vertical network can start with a single firm or with a group of firms, organizations, and professionals. A common factor is that members of a vertical network share strategic goals, vision, work plans, systems, policies, procedures, methodologies, and management information systems; participate in strategic planning sessions; jointly organize professional development training and annual meetings; and use common publications and training programs.

The majority of profit-oriented businesses and government organizations are examples of vertical strategic networks. Huge multinational corporations such as Microsoft, GE, Dell, and Procter & Gamble are obvious examples of vertical networks.

The Small Business Development Center program in the United States is an example of a vertical network within the public sector. Organized at the national level by the US Small Business Administration, the network has state centers communicating, collaborating, and co-ordinating with regional and local centers. The program is composed of business development consultants and state directors who strategize on and negotiate overall national, state and local program deliverables (e.g., number of consulting hours, number of clients served, number of training programs, etc.), and use common publications, tools, and training programs.

Strategic vertical networking can also occur between businesses in targeted sectors to collaborate or coalesce for greater international competitiveness, cost sharing, standardization, systematizing, and gathering strength through partnership. The telecommunications industry in Switzerland and the fruit processing industry in Brazil are but two of millions of examples of industries that could benefit from creating vertical networks.

Strategic Horizontal Networking

A strategic horizontal network may be less formal because it occurs among a variety of organizations that do not compete with one another but are rather in the same sphere of interest and influence. The intent of increased communication, collaboration, and coordination within this network is to reduce duplication and create standardization within an industry. However, goals, vision, work plans, systems, policies, procedures, and other ways of coordinating are usually not utilized because groups within the horizontal network are not administered or governed by one hierarchy or administrative structure.

As a result, and unfortunately, online communication, cooperation, professional development, shared goals, and carving of specific service-delivery niches does not occur too often in a horizontal network. For example, in the United States, One Stop Capital Shops, Women in

Business Centers, Export Assistance Centers, Chambers of Commerce, Service Corps of Retired Executives, Small Business Development Centers, Business Information Centers, private consulting firms, etc., offer similar programs and services within the horizontal network of common organizations. Yet they are limited by their lack of communication, co-operative agreements, and battles over "turf."

And, again, often charges of collusion and unfair competition are raised, keeping most firms from collaborating in a strategic horizontal network. But in industries where Internet, technology, and electronic commerce uses and applications are still in their infancy, the timeless phrase "united we stand, divided we fall" is *apropos* for these modern times.

To improve networking in general, and specifically foster greater e-commerce within an industry, a strategic planning process can be organized by using online communications technologies to create a shared vision and to identify how a sector will survive and thrive in an e-commerce marketplace. The difficulty for all sectors is planning a macro national strategy, keeping in mind micro or niche concerns (*a.k.a.* "turf" battles and secrecy) with participants in the network.

Assumptions about Networks

The following are some assumptions or "beliefs" about vertical, horizontal, formal, and informal networks that should be brought to your attention:

- Informal networks of firms, like-minded professionals, and sector-specific organizations communicating and collaborating between and among themselves are hugely important but not currently a reality of daily life. Creating more strategic, standardized, and coordinated networks at the horizontal and vertical levels are equally important. Yet they do not occur frequently in the private and public sectors. This is because many are blind to the advantages of sharing knowledge and contacts, collaborating on product development, contributing to improved efficiencies, ensuring higher and consistent standards, offering more standardized and consistent quality products, creating niches, reducing duplication of effort, price reductions, and loss of market share.
- Many networks do not have a formal coordinating body.

However, they are encouraged to establish one in order to improve communication and cooperation within a sector, develop industry-wide standards and systems for all to use, highlight best practices and successes, focus on professional development for the sector, and improve onsite and online service delivery.

- These networks can be "run like a business" and can be maintained through structured management and administration, memoranda of understanding, guidelines, action plans, and formal agreements between and among network partners.
- Often members of a network or community are not committed to the success of the group. That is, many network members belong to a network to receive information but do not nurture and build it through reciprocal sharing of ideas, information, best practices, or successful approaches and application of new technologies within a sector.
- Training and educating individuals within the network should be a primary concern of the strategic network to ensure an overall baseline level of knowledge, skills development, and technical competencies.

How Will You Know You've Succeeded?

A critical component of your e-commerce business strategy, your plan, is the method(s) by which you will know if you achieved your goals, if your tactics do what you think you want them to. If you don't measure where you are, you won't be able to tell where you're going and how far you've come—or not. Make an extensive and inclusive list of where you are now in terms of inquiries, sales by customer and region, promotion, staffing levels, shipping, record keeping, service requests, etc. Establish benchmarks. Establish a time line as to when and how often you will re-measure. Analyze the results so that you can fine tune as you move along.

So that you can evaluate the improvements and efficiencies gained after your e-commerce strategy and systems are implemented, the following is a list of suggested success factors for you to identify and then compare before, during, and after the establishment of your site:

- Increase in Gross Income (yes or no)
- Increase in Profit Margin (yes or no)
- Increase in Number of Employees (yes or no)
- Increase in Number of Customers (yes or no)

- Increase in Number of online Inquiries (yes or no)
- Increase in Staff Productivity (yes or no)
- Reduction in Number of Technical Problems (yes or no)
- Reduction in Production Costs (yes or no)
- Reduction in Administration Costs (yes or no)
- Increase in Technical Training for Staff (yes or no)
- Increase in Number of Customer Service Phone Calls (yes or no)
- Increase in Number of Customer Service E-mails (yes or no)
- Average Days to Respond to Inquiries (number before/number after)
- Reduction in the Number of Billing and Invoice Errors (yes or no)
- Integration of Software with Clients (yes or no)
- Most Popular Page on Your Web Site
- Least Visited Page on Your Web Site

Studies consistently find that firms with a clear e-commerce strategy generated a higher number of visits to the site. Regularly updating a site with useful information tends to foster repeat usage, but to attract new visitors, the ability to promote the site is of primary importance.

Importance of a Written E-Commerce Strategy

A well-defined and well-written strategy articulates goals, allocates resources, plans systems and processes, establishes a timetable and allows you to monitor results. You will need to determine who are to be involved, what level they occupy in the enterprise, and at what stages of the process they will be involved. Also determine who are to be the decision-makers and who will pull the plan together.

Through writing the plan, you will have a document that should enable you to spot "holes" in what you are considering, create a more systematic and efficient way of doing things, and reduce the risks and frustrations that are inevitable in this type of analysis and forward thinking. Keep in mind that it should be considered a flexible document, so that new information, changed directions, and additional elements can be incorporated.

You will also have, because of the comprehensiveness and thoroughness of your considerations, a better knowledge of your company— and yourself, your industry, and your product or services and its competitors.

**EXHIBIT 3.6 Basic Questions When Writing an
E-Commerce Strategy**

Do you/Will you . . .

   Have an operating site?

   Update the site at least monthly?

   Have links to related sites?

   Include your company address, telephone and fax numbers, and e-mail
      address prominently?

   Provide the names and e-mail addresses of key staff?

   Provide profiles and photographs of these people?

   Know that most users can find what they need in three clicks or less?

   Use CRM software to archive, monitor, and respond to visitors' questions and
      preferences? And analyze the aggregate activities?

   Make your privacy policy clear?

   Specifically ask permission to share client names and other information?

   Conduct ongoing focus groups of your customers' online needs?

   Offer online services or activitie in response to client needs?

   Acknowledge orders placed and promote sales or special incentives once a
      season?

   Allow clients to share information on message boards or in chat rooms?

   Offer shopping carts for online purchasing?

   Offer messaging or immediate telephone call-backs from a real person?

   Answer all e-mail within 24 hours?

   Send e-mail newsletters once a month to clients and customers?

   Have the ability to can handle a large increase in volume as a result of online
      sales?

   Meet regularly with your Web designer to keep him or her current with your
      overall corporate strategy?

Basic E-Commerce Strategic Plan

The following is an outline of a basic e-commerce strategy which, of
course, should be customized to your situation.

Executive Summary. Brief statement of the products manufactured,
what makes the firm successful, advantages over competitors, and goals
for the next five years. State what makes your business better than competitors that already have a presence on the Internet.

History of the Company. Date founded, revenue and profit history,
growth and contraction of number of employees, product diversification

as the company expanded, successes, challenges, etc. Describe how it changed over time. Describe its successes, frustrations, and expectations for future e-commerce opportunities. Explain when the company will adopt its Internet presence.

Current Company Profile. Summary of products manufactured, organization chart or "organigram," and the major projects achieved last year and planned for the next five years.

Mission Statement/Goals. What you hope to achieve by having a good Internet presence and how you will measure the success of these goals.

Prospects for Growth. Competitive advantages (why is the product unique?), competitive challenges (what could threaten the profitability of the company?), and competitive opportunities (what are the factors that could increase the growth of the company?). Identify the products and services that will sell well over the Internet and give the reasons why. State also why you expect growth from having an online presence.

Industry Trends. Describe the opportunities for e-commerce in your industry. How has the Internet and ICT changed your industry? What are the expected trends in your industry for e-commerce?

Competition. Who are your main competitors and why are they considered competitors (e.g., better product, bigger market share, found in more locations and/or countries, greater name recognition)? List the Web sites of major and minor competitors. What is the estimated market share of each competitor? Are they increasing market share through having an online commerce strategy and a dynamic site?

Strategic Approach. Explain the strategic approach that was selected for e-commerce activities. State how the e-commerce strategy will be incorporated—integrated—into the company. Describe how interactions with customers will change. Describe how you will gain your customers' trust. Describe how efficiencies will be created. Describe your vertical and/or horizontal networking activity. Describe how you will measure the results of your going online.

Management and Staff. Profiles of company president/CEO and its directors, and a sample of rising stars within the company. Emphasize their experience and background in e-commerce system design, ICT, marketing, and online sales. Include how staff responsibilities will change now that you will have an e-commerce strategy.

Current Customers. Who are they, where are they located, what industries are they in, and how did you get them? Ask customers what they need from you in terms of the Internet, your site, and integration of information and communication technology. Why do you believe they will purchase from you over the Internet?

Target Markets. Clear definitions of the markets with all their characteristics and components. Compare them with the profile of current customers. (Keep in mind that smaller companies should examine the markets that large corporations either overlook or consider too small to be profitable.)

Pricing Strategy. Summary of pricing strategies for your target markets in comparison to the competition. Will the product be priced higher or lower or the same? Why? Explain your pricing strategy for selling and buying online. Will your prices be different from offline sales? On what basis?

Distribution. Who will handle the distribution and shipping of the product? How will new ICT and integrated systems change previous distribution systems?

Promotional Strategy. Summary of direct mail; print, radio, television, advertising; publicity; telephone cold calling or on-site visits; trade shows; e-mail; Internet, and other means of promotion. Summary of the countries or regions in which the marketing campaign will take place. Show how you intend to attract online customers, importers, agents, distributors, and how their interest in e-commerce will be sustained. How can you convince them to buy from you online?

Customer Service. Summary of after-sales service plans, establishment of customer service center, and overall plans to keep the customer satisfied. How will new ICT and integrated customer management information systems change or improve your service to customers?

Manufacturing Plan. Number of units to be produced, source of materials, location of manufacturing sites, and the challenges, changes, and risks foreseen as a result of your new e-commerce strategy.

Budget. Total annual cost of operation including personnel, rent, equipment, billing system, marketing, travel, etc., as a result of your new e-commerce strategy.

Financial Projections. Cash flow or annual total revenue anticipated against total costs or budgeted expenses as a result of your new e-commerce strategy.

Break-Even Analysis. Total number of units to be sold to make neither a profit nor a loss.

Source of Financing. From where will adequate financing come to initiate and sustain the e-commerce operations?

Distribution of Profit/Expansion Plans. Summary of where profits are planned to be distributed for company expansion.

A final word of caution here about strategy before we move on to the execution of strategy. Senior management of businesses often tends to give up control of their e-commerce strategy. When they do, it's left to young, energetic, technically savvy and well-intentioned lower management employees with no strategic, marketing, or financial management experience. The result is that they eventually, sooner or later, clash with upper management. Then everyone becomes not only frustrated with the lack of performance, but remain confounded, confused, or unwilling to invest the time needed to fully understand this phenomenon.

4

Five Cs of Successful E-Commerce Web Sites

As mentioned earlier, there are several forms of electronic commerce. The most prevailing, persistent, and potentially perishable are the sites on the Internet. Thus we focus here on what makes an Internet site successful—or not—from the points of view of both the enterprise and those it wants to do business with. Enterprises *are* finding that the Internet is a relatively low-cost tool for marketing their products and services both locally and globally.

Winning Web Sites

So, what makes a site successful? How do you design viable and effective sites for increased sales and marketing? Among other things, the site must be easily navigable, managed closely by senior management, and updated with new services and promotions. This means fast-loading pages, product specifications, pertinent information, and easy-to-understand prices. Responses to customer e-mail queries are made within 24 hours, key words are carefully selected for indexing by search engines, and links are made to related sites. Information on the company is provided, including an employee listing with phone numbers and e-mail addresses. These components seem obvious, yet one or more are all too often not incorporated into the site.

Most important, a good site must help the user meet a need, in all of its ramifications, whether the need is for information about your products or your company, for making purchasing convenient, or even for entertainment.

Are We Listening to the Customer?

Until businesses truly understand how corporate buyers and consumers prefer to use technology and the Internet in their business and personal lives, we are going to see a turbulent technology market with small percentages actually using the Internet for business purposes.

Every business must be able to show that it has understood the customer's viewpoint, achieved through intensive and time-consuming endeavors such as focus groups with customers and beta testing of the marketing, customer support, financial, transactional, and technological aspects of the site.

Unfortunately, senior managers and their software developers consistently try to create one integrated client database (for customer service purposes, for example), only to have employees ignore it because of its complexity and/or they think it is giving away too much information to co-workers. Only half the employees know how to use it. And, also unfortunately, many managers of businesses who would have a heart attack if their phone lines were down for ten seconds, think nothing of letting an online customer wait days for an e-mail reply.

These are just a few small examples of why people are circumspect about and hesitant to use technology and the Internet. Most software turns traditional and comfortable hierarchies, information fiefdoms, and communication methods upside down. Most Internet sites just don't satisfy our need to know and our need to buy on our own terms (offering us both "wow and now").

Nonthreatening technological applications for and responsive customer service on the Internet is just in its infancy and businesses that realize this now will be the victors in the marketplace.

What Makes a Site Successful?

As noted, a successful commercial site gives value to the business as well as its customers. Therefore, any site expenditure that does not return value to the business is over-expenditure. To obtain value from your site, and avoid over-expenditure, you must carefully define what functions you expect the site to perform, ensure that those functions are carried out efficiently, and make your site highly visible to your target markets.

Earning a Customer's Trust

At the heart of success is the trust of your customers. Here are some ways you can build that trust in the unfamiliar, exciting, and potentially huge realm of e-commerce.

Tell Customers Who/Where You Are. Display your company name street address (or postal box number), and city and state (or province) on your home page, along with phone and fax numbers and e-mail addresses, even if it is smaller print compared to the main "show." Consumers like having different methods to contact companies. Unfortunately, some sites don't have even *any* of the above ways to contact a company.

Provide Detailed Product and Service Information. Because online shoppers cannot inspect your wares, you should offer as much detailed information as you can about your products and services. Describe them in simple language, emphasizing benefits, not just the features.

Provide Customers with a Clear, Multistep Purchasing Process. Set up a separate screen for an order form or a shopping cart that allows consumers to identify the items they are thinking about buying. As they select an item, they send it to a "shopping cart." They then can view the items in the cart before clicking on the send button to finalize their order. If you do not have a multistep purchasing process, you should provide a period during which customers can change their minds. Show full prices, terms and conditions, and transaction methods.

Allow a Quick-buy Option for Repeat Customers. Repeat customers may want a convenient way to order products. A quick-buy feature provides customers with a clear and simple purchasing process for future orders.

Provide Clear Terms and Conditions. Indicate full prices, the currency in which prices are calculated and to be paid, shipping charges, taxes, customs duties, customs brokerage fees, delivery schedules. Also state your return and exchange policies.

Tell Customers About the Security of Your Transaction System. State who provides the security and how it works.

Post a Privacy Policy on Your Site. Review the privacy policies that are already on many sites. Hewlett Packard (HP), Compaq, Hotmail, Amazon and many other sites require—and store—personal information on their customers and post their policies regarding the use of such private information.

Have Your Site Certified. One way to reassure consumers is to have a reputable third party endorse your business. A number of Internet approval programs are emerging. They range from those that simply verify that your business exists at its claimed address to those that provide comprehensive auditing services.

Respond to Customer Complaints. Provide a simple and effective process for handling customer complaints, concerns, and inquiries. Third-party dispute-resolution services can act as mediators or arbitrators.

The Five Cs of Successful Sites

Think of developing your site in terms of the following tips, categorized by five easy-to-remember Cs: clarity, content, convenience, commerce, and commitment.

Clarity

- Use the company name and logo, with colors used throughout that match the logo.
- Use few colors, contrasting colors, keeping in mind the combinations that confuse the color-blind.
- Use "clean," simple, and consistent graphics.
- Use minimal graphics and photos to save on downloading time.
- Keep the background uncluttered.
- Use a typeface that is easy to read—and use only one or two typestyles, in only two or three sizes.
- Use short sentences, short paragraphs, with "action" words that can easily be understood.
- Keep your site simple—with all pertinent information, but no superfluous information. Figure out your basic information architecture first, then the finishing details.
- Design logical, sequential navigation through pages—and an easy way to get back again.
- Limit animation, except when movement will show different angles of a product.
- Provide a navigation bar at the top of each page to provide constant access to the key areas of the site.

Content

- Briefly describe your products and the company on the first (home) page.
- Include your mailing address, telephone and fax numbers, e-mail addresses.
- Describe and show exactly what the business does and the services it provides in terms of customer benefits.
- Use key words that customers intuitively use to find your site.

- Clearly indicate the categories of products for sale on your site.
- Give tips on how to make use of the site.
- Answer frequently asked questions (FAQs).
- Include any policies and procedures that are important to know.
- Include warranty information.
- Include a user manual, if appropriate.
- Provide information on company services and staff—and how to contact them.
- Include quality awards.
- Provide links to other useful sites related to your industry.
- List job opportunities and how to apply for them.
- List major customers (with their permission) who are using your product(s)—and how—along with their contact information or links to their sites.
- Allow individual divisions to update their own sections in keeping with company guidelines, instead of relying on a Web designer.
- Require updates at least four times a year.

Convenience

- Offer more than one language on the site, particularly the language of your targeted clientele.
- List locations where your product is available.
- Allow items to be searchable by product, sector, and country.
- Allow registration of visitors to the site.
- Highlight new developments on the site.
- Provide country-specific market reports.
- Direct users to where favorite pages can be found.
- Alert users when specific auctions are posted on the site or within your industry.
- Offer a "want ads" section for clients.
- Provide industry analysis, glossary, and compare global specifications.
- Offer an online magazine.
- Post news releases.
- Provide useful information for students, teachers, and young professionals.
- Provide daily market news, statistics, and prices.

Commerce

- Allow buyers to search the site through internal search engines.
- Have buyers click through no more than three times in order to find needed information.
- Allow buyers to save information for future visits.
- Ensure that the price is easy to calculate for your client.
- Include a privacy statement, if you have the ability to conduct transactions.
- Include a brief section on how to do business with your company, if appropriate.
- Provide financing information, if appropriate.
- Consider offering free shipping.
- Instead of having payments made only online by credit card, offer direct debit or billing options.
- Allow customers to view details of prior purchases.
- Allow customers to review intended purchases and to modify orders before completing a purchase.
- Provide a secure encryption service so users can transmit sensitive information through the Internet.
- Indicate that an order confirmation will be sent by e-mail.
- Show what's "on sale."
- Include sections for buyer- and seller-related information.
- List proposed projects, contracts, and bids to alert your users to business opportunities.
- Allow users to search for Requests for Tenders (RFTs), Requests for Quotations (RFQs), or Requests for Proposals (RFPs) for products and services you wish to purchase.
- Offer a secure online system for RFQs for purchases from suppliers.

Customer Commitment

- Offer toll-free "live" 24-hour assistance from experts, using telephone, e-mail, or instant messaging.
- Promise to respond fully within one to three business days.
- Allow customers to compare price, terms of payment, service, delivery schedules.
- Make it as easy as possible for a customer to return a purchase.
- Provide customer-friendly shipment, billing, and delivery options.

- Allow customers to check their order status online.
- Offer tutorials on technical matters to make it easier to use your product, your site.
- Allow customers to provide feedback about their experience on the site.
- Allow customers to review and rate your services.
- Make reviews and ratings available to other customers.
- Include an online questionnaire seeking specific information on how the site can be improved.
- Have a "first time visitor" button.
- Provide online information, education, training, and other need-to-know information.
- Offer an interesting, useful screen saver on your business for clients.
- Give the customer the option to use an auction or buyer's bid.
- Host a virtual conference or informal discussion on selected topics.
- Encourage debate, the sharing of ideas and discussion of ideas among your customers.
- Offer free services for buyers and sellers.
- To create trust among trading partners, give buyers and sellers a list of members.
- If you have a marketplace, highlight prominent members and the new members.
- Users who provide testimonials should receive a discount, product, etc.

Primary Areas of E-Commerce

The use of e-commerce varies considerably. Exhibit 4.1 highlights the primary areas of e-commerce and brief descriptions of each follow. They include business-to-business (B2B) and business-to-government (B2G) sites for supplier and procurement opportunities. Others include sites for retail sales (B2C), price comparisons by industry (C2B), and traditional and reverse auctions (B2B and C2C).

Business-to-Business/B2B Web Sites
SUPPLIER/BUSINESS SERVICES SITES

Jupiter MMXI defines three key success criteria for B2B sites as follows: (1) a high volume of transactions; (2) significant experience and backing

---

EXHIBIT 4.1 Primary Areas of E-Commerce

	Business	**Government**	**Consumer**
Business	Supply Opportunities Auctions Reverse Auctions	Procurement Opportunities	Retail Sales
Government	E-Government / Advocacy on Regulatory, Tax Free Trade Issues	Standardization of International Trade	E-Government
Consumer	Price Comparisons Customer Care	Complaints Paying Taxes Questions	Auctions / Opinions on Products

---

Source: McCue.

from the company's industry; and (3) integration of online offerings with offline services such as full telephone service and local customer support.

Business-to-Government/B2G Web Sites
PROCUREMENT WEB SITES

B2G sites provide businesses with easy access to government current tenders, offers, agency contracts, and governmental procurement policies at international, regional, national, and local levels.

Business-to-Consumer/B2C Web Sites
RETAIL/SERVICE SITES

B2C sites sell products or services directly to individual consumers. These sites usually offer the opportunity for a buyer to submit credit card information to the site so that purchase order information is quickly and securely processed.

Government-to-Business/G2B Web Sites
ECONOMIC DEVELOPMENT SITES, INCLUDING
TAX AND REGULATORY COMPLIANCE

G2B sites provide statistical information for business planning purposes as well as information on training programs and counseling services.

They also usually include lists of buyers of goods and RFQs, online publications, and contact information for various ministries. They may also include public and private sector associations that assist enterprises in penetrating local, national, and international markets.

Government-to-Government/G2G Web Sites
WEB SITES FOR GOVERNMENT STANDARDS, PROTOCOLS, LEGISLATION

G2G sites typically provide links to other similar governmental institutions; publish safety, packaging and other conformity standards for a particular region, country, or sector; and provide information on the programs offered by governmental organizations at the international (United Nations), national, regional, and local levels.

Government-to-Consumer/G2C Web Sites
E-GOVERNMENT SITES

G2C sites enable governments to provide citizens with many types of need-to-know information such as government reports and statistics, forms, publications, contact information for various ministries, and information alerts.

Consumer-to-Business/C2B Web Sites
PRICE COMPARISON WEB SITES

C2B sites allow for price comparison on products offered by retailers or distributors. The consumer is usually able to search for products throughout the country or the world. These sites may also allow consumers to submit their "ratings" or impressions of a product that they have recently used or purchased. These types of sites allow consumers to bid on a product or service, indicating a price they are willing to pay instead of accepting a published price.

Consumer-to-Government/C2G Web Sites
REGULATORY AND TAX COMPLIANCE WEB SITES

C2G sites allow citizens to interact with government officials and bureaucrats via the Internet. Essentially, these sites enable citizens and businesses to meet their obligations and conform to government rules and regulations online. For example, citizens can submit tax returns, vote in elections, and send comments to elected and appointed officials—all online. These opportunities may be built into the C2G site.

Consumer-to-Consumer/C2C Web Sites

AUCTION OR ADVOCACY SITES

C2C sites are usually auction or advocacy sites that provide the latest news or contact information for a particular industry sector, buyer's guides, statistics, and the ability to purchase product and services through increasingly popular online auctions.

Category Killer Web Sites

OTHER GREAT SITES

Category killer sites are simply other great sites that make using the Internet efficient, cost-effective, or educational or increase communication opportunities for citizens and businesses around the world.

101 Winning Web Sites

The best way to improve your chances for success is by learning from those who have taken the risk to increase their own marketing reach and improve their profitability by using ICT and the Internet.

The examples below were selected from hundreds of sites that Prima de Sousa and I analyzed in 2001 by the International Trade Center (ITC), a cooperating agency of the United Nations Conference and Trade and Development and the World Trade Organization. They were chosen based on the criteria of clarity, content, convenience, commerce, and commitment to customer and on the primary areas of e-commerce.

They are exemplary sites, grouped into ten sections with at least ten examples each primary area of e-commerce. Note that they are sites based all over the world. After all, e-commerce remains an emerging and changing phenomenon in all countries and in all industries. Check them out. Analyze them. You will probably find one or more elements that you will be able to adopt/adapt to the benefit of your site. If any of these sites no longer exists, you may view them by going to the Internet archives at www.archive.org.

Business-to-Business/B2B Web Sites

PORTALS AND SUPPLIER / BUSINESS SERVICES SITES

Acequote / http://www.acequote.com. This site facilitates online procurement and sourcing of materials. It matches buyers with suppliers of information technology products, services, and technology. A highlight of the site is its online technical support available via e-mail.

Buildonline / http://www.buildonline.com. This multilingual marketplace provides Internet-based project management and catalog software for the construction industry in seven European countries. The site offers news, industry research, a recruitment database, and financial and credit services. New customers are offered training on how to use the site.

Coffee Exchange / http://www.coffee-exchange.com. This comprehensive coffee-trading portal provides an international database of coffee producers. It allows for searching by key word, country, or company. It offers online price quotes, charts, auctions, discussion forums, related industry news information, currency exchange rates, and a job exchange board.

Cyber Celler / http://www.cybercellar.co.za. The site promotes South African wines through its portal, auction, or marketplace. Information on wines available for sale is arranged by category (e.g., red, white, sparkling, or fortified). A five-star rating system ranges from "plain and simple" to "a Caper classic." Wines for auction include a description and rating.

DoveBid / http://www.dovebid.com. This auction site hosts heavy manufacturing equipment auctions that are conducted online and through live Web casts. Links to transaction support services such as valuations, shipping, and escrow services.

EPlastics / http://www.eplasticsindia.com. Designed for the plastics industry in India, this site actually encompasses the global market. It includes a trading floor where buyers and sellers can exchange products, a searchable directory, lists of licensed producers, sales cooperatives, and technology transfer.

Farm World / http://www.farmworld.com. The site provides a list of farm products producers by general groupings (e.g., grains, oil seeds, citrus fruits, garden vegetables). Each group is linked to another page for a more specific product breakdown of the groupings, such as oranges, grapefruits, and pineapples for citrus fruits.

GoIndustry / http://www.goindustry.com. This is a marketplace offering construction industry auctions, news, industry research, recruitment databases, and financial services. GoIndustry contacts the highest bidder by e-mail and allows customers two business days to confirm the offer.

LeatherIndia / http://www.leatherindia.com. Designed for leather importers and exporters based in India, the site provides news links, price quotes, and a directory of importers. It allows for a search by product category or country. Companies profiled in the directory list company certifications, turnover, years in business, and specific products offered. The site also offers informational resources such as a currency converter, country profiles, leather events and fairs. It also has links for language translation.

MetalSite / http://www.metalsite.com. An online exchange of metals, the site provides logistics planning and credit services. It offers services that cover all aspects of a transaction, from inquiry to payment. The opening page highlights sellers that use the exchange. Customer service is available 24 hours a day, accessible through a global toll-free number, fax, e-mail, and live Internet support.

Oryza / http://www.oryza.com. The site provides real-time trading for the global rice industry. Market reports and a daily e-mail newsletter are free. Credit verification, freight and logistics, payment guarantee, inspection, insurance and shipment tracking are available to paying members.

PackagingNetwork / http://www.packagingnetwork.com. This is an online store and auction house for packaging materials and equipment, industry news and regulations. The site contains a useful navigation bar at the top of each page that provides constant access to five key areas of the site. To facilitate interaction among packaging professionals, the news and community section hosts virtual conferences on selected topics.

Procure Steel / http://www.procuresteel.com. The site allows online trading for steel, brass, copper, aluminum, and plastics. The site allows only buyers and sellers to post their needs and the posting of company contact information with a link to the site of the registered company. Any sales are conducted outside of the portal, or "offline." Bulletin boards are organized by product topics: Material Needed, Steel for Sale, Fabricator, Equipment, Freight, and Information.

Recycle Auction Group / http://www.ragauction.com. Open exchange for buying and selling recyclable materials. Users are alerted when specific auctions occur.

Rice Trader / http://www.ricetradecenter.com. Rice Trader is an informational portal and a free online database. Users may search by company name or by country.

Rubber Commerce / http://www.rubbercommerce.com. Serving the rubber industry, this portal provides an online exchange, resources, information, and services. The user may link into five different exchanges for raw materials, machinery, tires, instruments, and general rubber products.

Tea Auction / http://www.teauction.com. One of the most technologically-advanced portals, this site is wireless access point (WAP)-enabled. It also provides an array of services to its users. It includes a vocabulary, glossary, directory, statistics on the global tea market, shipping companies, online payment system, weekly auction, free e-mail service, newsletter, and access to a tea expert available to answer questions.

Textile Solutions / http://www.textilesolutions.com. Designed for the textile industry, this site offers the elements and services necessary to complete an onsite transaction, including suppliers, buyers, quality checks, credit ratings, payment and logistics arrangements.

Timber Africa / http://www.timberafrica.com. Based in South Africa, this timber-trading portal caters to the "South African Pine" market. It provides a place for buyers and sellers to meet and exchange products. The site is secured; buyers and sellers must submit an online registration form before participating. After the form is submitted, the buyer/seller will receive an e-mail with their login and password to access the trading floor. Through a partnership with American Express and other companies, users are able to move entirely through the process of a transaction on the site.

TimberWeb / http://www.timberWeb.com. This is a fee-based marketplace for timber and wood products, with three levels of membership. Available are services such as industry news, online networking, and access to a directory of 200,000 businesses. It is easy for members and related groups to create links to the site. With a dynamic "request for quotation" system to purchase, the site has an "eTrader" platform that creates legally binding "eContracts" so that traders can conclude deals online. The site also offers a monitored message board for members.

Wood Center / http://www.woodcenter.net. This French/English site serves as a portal for wood products, paper, packing, and lumber products. It allows searches by keyword or product category (e.g., wood product, processing, paper, etc.). After you submit the keyword, a list of firms appears with hyperlinks to their sites along with a brief text description.

World of Fruit / http://www.worldoffruit.com. With users from over 35 countries, this site serves as a marketplace for the fresh fruit and vegetable industry. The site provides two marketplace services: the "fruitXchange" and the "fruitAuction." Companies must have been trading for at least one year and have a turnover higher than one million euros in order to register to trade on the site.

Yet2 / http://www.yet2.com. The site is a cross-industry marketplace for buying, selling, and licensing patents, technology, and technical information. Technology owners describe their licensable discoveries on the site, and buyers post want ads to see if someone has developed the technology needed. It helps companies, individuals, and government agencies to reduce research and development costs. Registration is free, but users pay a commission if a transaction occurs as a result of an introduction on the site.

Business-to-Government/B2G Web Sites
PROCUREMENT WEB SITES

ADB Business Opportunities / http://www.adb.org/business. The Asian Development Bank funds development programs in Asia and the Pacific regions, generating business opportunities for businesses in member countries. The site contains a guide on doing business with ADB and answers frequently asked questions. A "Business Center" contains information on projects and contract awards to alert contractors to potential business opportunities.

African Development Bank / http://www.afdb.org/opportunities/. Procurement opportunities are listed by country and sector. Procedures to apply for contract opportunities are clearly explained.

BCBid / http://www.bcbid.ca. The government of British Columbia offers opportunities for suppliers of goods and services. These tenders are downloadable by date, classification, ministry or service. Registered users can subscribe to a bid notification service wherein they are notified by e-mail of opportunities.

BGConsulting / http://www.bg-consulting.com. This consulting firm advises on public policy in Latin American countries and links these countries with international development agencies. Publications are available by e-mail once payment is received.

Botswana Tenders / http://www.gov.bw.business/tenders.html. Tenders are issued by government ministries. After completing an online registration form, businesses can download tenders from the site.

DPWS / http://www.tenders.dpws.nsw.gov.au/dpws/. The site of the Department of Public Works and Services of New South Wales in Australia contains proposed, current, recently closed, and awarded tenders, listed by category and by close date. Useful search engine facilitates finding requests for tenders (RFTs).

Electronic Tendering System / http://www.ets.com.hk. Free services of the Hong Kong Special Administrative Region's Government Supplies Department (GSD) include publication of tenders, contract award notices, and general terms and conditions for GSD tenders. Users must pay a registration fee to access certain services, including a 12-month forecast of planned purchases for government departments.

Government Electronic Tenders Service / http://www.gets.govt.nz. This site provides procurement opportunities through the New Zealand Industrial Supplies Office. A "tender watch" alerts suppliers to new opportunities.

Inter-Agency Procurement Services Office / http://www.iapso.org. Part of the United Nations Development Program, this site provides alerts on UN agencies, non-profit organizations, and donor agencies. Provides a database of prospective suppliers, allows registration to become a UN supplier, and has a small training program on UN procurement procedures.

SIMAP / http://www.simap.eu.int. Available in 11 languages, this site provides links to procurement opportunities across the European Union, and offers discussion fora on how to improve procurement skills.

Business-to-Consumer/B2C Web Sites
RETAIL / SERVICE SITES

Amazon / http://www.amazon.com. Regarded by many as a pioneer in Internet B2C e-commerce, the site began as an online-only bookstore and has diversified into music, electronics, software, health and beauty, etc. Potential customers can review and rate books on the site. Repeat customers receive personalized product recommendations based on their prior purchases. Shipment, billing, and delivery options are very customer-friendly.

CatalyseInt / http://www.catalyse-int.com. This e-commerce strategy consulting firm's site offers uncluttered presentation, few colors, and simple graphics. Information about the company's services and employees is provided. Prospective clients may submit an online query to the firm.

CliffsNotes / http://www.cliffsnotes.com. This site is a sales and marketing site for CliffsNotes, a student study aid that provides summaries of classic books. For a fee, CliffsNotes can be downloaded from the site or delivered by mail in hard copy. The site also includes tips for students on writing and employment interview techniques. A useful marketing technique is its free newsletter sent to registered users each week. Users who provide testimonials receive a free download and have their messages posted on the site.

EasyJet / http://www.easyjet.com. This site is a successful European online-only provider of short haul airline ticket, car rental, and hotel bookings. In a few clicks and minimal time, the customer is able to find needed information.

EIU / http://www.eiu.com. The site provides fee-based economic information, research, and analysis by *The Economist's* Intelligence Unit. It contains several links to related sites of interest to business professionals. The site hosts a free Ebusinessforum which contains e-commerce news, analysis, and interactive features such as an e-poll and e-discussions.

Expertcity / http://www.expertcity.com. ExpertLive is the site's on-line marketplace where experts provide 24-hour "live" solutions to consumers' software, hardware, or programming problems. Users can select an expert based on price, resume, rating, or member comments. Users can search for experts by topic or keywords. Customers pay, by credit card, only if they are satisfied with the service received.

LebanonShop / http://www.lebanonshop.com. A Lebanese online shopping mall, it offers antiques, books, crafts, and music with prices quoted in US dollars. Featured products, displayed with photo and price are updated regularly. Product categories are listed in a helpful navigation bar, and shipping is free anywhere in the world.

LeShop / http://www.leshop.ch. This online-only grocery store offers home delivery in Switzerland. The site allows consumers to refer to prior purchases. All products are pictured, and are listed with the price and a short description that includes ingredients. Special offers and new products are listed separately, making them easier to find. Customers can pay by direct debit from a Swiss account, or by credit card, or they can be billed.

PhotoDisc / http://www.photodisc.com. The site offers online sales from a collection of 90,000 photographs. Images in the database are catalogd by keyword and number, providing an easy search.

Rolex / http://www.rolex.com. The site provides information on the company, its products, distributors, and information on corporate-sponsored sporting and cultural events. Benefiting from the Internet's reach to a global audience, the company uses its site only for marketing purposes. Internet sales are not permitted.

Government-to-Business/G2B Web Sites

ECONOMIC DEVELOPMENT SITES INCLUDING TAX AND REGULATORY COMPLIANCE

Bancomext / http://www.bancomext.com. Available in Spanish and English, the site provides foreign trade statistics, investment opportunities in Mexico, and a directory of exporters categorized by industry. The site is divided into two main categories: trade information (exporters' directories, market statistics, lists of publications) and trade development (export tenders, counseling, and training for exporters). E-mail-based client support is provided.

Business Referral and Information Network / http://www.brain. org.za. Initiated by the South African Department of Trade and Industry and international development agencies, this site assists small businesses in becoming internationally competitive. The site contains information on financing, training, and planning and running a small business. It offers referrals to other business-support organizations.

China External Trade Development Council / http://www.cetra. org.tw/. Taiwan's Virtual Trade Mart features products from 38,000 companies and a section on doing business in Taiwan. Local users can find national business news and dates of trade shows.

ChinaProducts / http://www.chinaproducts.com. This Chinese trade portal contains trade leads, legal, economic, and business news. It contains a separate section for trade, ranking the top 20 products and/or companies within a specific industry.

EMarket Services / http://www.emarketservices.com. This site is a portal to Internet B2B marketplaces, organized by an international collaboration of trade development organizations. The site also contains news and information about conferences and research to raise awareness of e-marketplaces. Marketplaces are searchable by name or industry category.

Japan External Trade Organization / / http://www.jetro.go.jp. The site provides information for exporters to Japan and foreign investors in Japan. Frequent updates encourage users to return to it as a reliable and current information source.

Latvian Development Agency / http://www.lad.gov.lv. Online services include postings of business opportunities, highlights of Latvian business sectors for foreign investors, and legal and regulatory requirements for doing business in Latvia.

Metro Electronic Trade Center / http://www.tradepretoria.co.za. Information on doing business in South Africa is arranged for foreign traders and domestic companies. It also includes guides on exporting, market surveys, and links to counseling and training organizations.

National Association of Automobile Manufacturers in South Africa / http://www.naamsa.co.za. Auto sector news and statistics are provided for manufacturers, assemblers, importers, and distributors of automobiles.

UK Online for Business / http://www.ukonlineforbusiness.gov.uk. Part of the United Kingdom's national e-commerce strategy, the site provides advice to enterprises about using information and communication technology through research, case studies, and events. The site is organized into "business advice," displaying sources of advice and training and "business benefits," showcasing case studies and international research.

United States Department of Commerce / http://www.doc.gov. A vast site for US firms seeking to export, it includes guides, lists of export opportunities, and links to government organizations. Users benefit from basic, intermediate, and advanced search engines.

Government-to-Government/G2G Web Sites
WEB SITES FOR GOVERNMENT STANDARDS, PROTOCOLS, LEGISLATION

European Organization for Conformity Assessment / http://www.eotc.be. EOTC members are national and European agencies that attempt to ensure that products and services meet required specifications. An interactive help desk provides information on conformity assessment to users, and e-discussions are hosted regularly.

The European Union Online / http://www.europa.eu.int. The site provides links to EU institutions including the parliament, Court of Auditors, and Central Bank. It also has official documents. Each section of the site has a specific e-mail address to reduce the time that users must wait for assistance.

Food and Agriculture Organization / http://www.fao.org. FAO focuses on agriculture, forestry, fisheries, and rural development. The site publishes departmental magazines, guides, statistical databases, and explanations of the organization's programs. It includes a comprehensive photo library.

International Organization for Standardization / http://www.iso.ch. ISO is a network of national standards institutes from 140 countries working in partnership with governments, industry, business, and consumer representatives. Publications are delivered as paper copies or sent electronically within twenty-four hours.

International Telecommunications Union / http://www.itu.int. ITU helps governments and the private sector coordinate global telecom networks and services. The site provides information on councils and regulatory boards including the Telecommunication Information Exchange Service. An online subscription for publications is offered.

International Trade Center / http://www.intracen.org. ITC is a technical cooperation agency of the United Nations Conference on Trade and Development and the World Trade Organization for operational, enterprise-oriented aspects of trade development. The ITC posts its excellent quarterly magazine, International Trade Forum, and archived virtual conferences.

Organization for Economic Co-operation and Development / http://www.oecd.org. The OECD is comprised of 30 member countries that share a commitment to democracy and a market economy. The site includes its magazine, policy briefs, ministerial meeting reports and research papers. New users can find popular sections of the site by clicking on "most visited pages."

United Nations / http://www.un.org. The UN seeks to maintain international peace and security, develop friendly relations among nations, cooperate in solving international problems, promote respect for human rights, and serve at the center of harmonizing actions of nations. The UN site organizes a very large amount of information in a well-structured manner.

The World Bank / http://www.worldbank.org. The World Bank Group is made up of five organizations whose mission is to fight poverty and to help people help themselves and their environment by providing resources, sharing knowledge, and forging partnerships. A "speaker's corner" provokes debate on development issues and the "development forum" hosts e-discussions on key issues and challenges facing the development community.

World Trade Organization / http://www.wto.org. The WTO focuses on the rules of trade between nations, administers trade agreements, and serves as a forum for negotiations between governments, with the aim to help producers of goods and services to conduct trade. The site contains sections for trade specialists, general public, students, and academics. A downloadable training package is also available.

Government-to-Consumer/G2C Web Sites

E-GOVERNMENT SITES

Government of Canada / http://www.canada.gc.ca. Information and services provided to Canadian citizens include government forms, health care reports, and information on services for people with disabilities, etc. Provides contact information for in-person government assistance.

Government of Ireland / http://www.gov.ie/. This site serves as a portal, enabling users to find government departments of information about Ireland, including links to government organizations. Information is provided on citizenship, taxes, employment, family, education, housing, business, and statistics.

Health and Safety Executive / http://www.hse.gov.uk/. The site seeks to ensure that risks to health and safety-related work activities are controlled. It includes a public register of successful prosecutions undertaken, inquiry reports on accidents, etc. An "incident center" allows users to report accidents and diseases online.

Metropolitan Manila Development Authority / http://www. mmda.gov.ph/index.shtml. Local government site of Manila that has responsibility for development planning, transport and traffic management, food control, waste disposal, zoning and land use planning, etc. The goal of the site is to service the information needs of the public in its jurisdiction. An online hotline enables citizens to complain and make suggestions.

Ministry of Environment and Natural Resources / http://www. mec.go.ke/index.html. This Kenyan ministry provides information about Kenya's biodiversity conservation program. Ressearchers can find Kenya's national biodiversity strategy as well as details of specific projects in Kenya.

Ministry of Trade and Industry / http://www.mti.gov.nal. This Namibian ministry site provides information on trade, industrial development, investment, trade fairs, and full contact information for relevant ministry officials.

Procuraduria General de la Republico / http://www.pgr.gob.mx. Mexico's public prosecution office provides information on national crime prevention policies, lists most wanted criminals, and offers downloadable posters of missing persons.

Presidency of the Dominican Republic / http://www.presidencia. gov.do. The site provides profiles of the president and cabinet members, news, and reports. It has an online complaint line.

Republic of Bulgaria / http://www.government.bg. The site contains news from the government, national strategies, draft legislation, and the "dialogue 2002" electronic debate on the government's development program.

United States Census Bureau / http://www.census.gov. Contains analyses of population and business data, including data from the 2000 census. The information, although complex, is nicely organized for use by laypersons and professionals. A "new on the site" section allows repeat users to know what has been added in the past 30 days.

Consumer-to-Business/C2B Web Sites

PRICE COMPARISON WEB SITES

AddALL / http://www.addall.com. This book search and price comparison site allows buyers to compare prices from more than 40 online bookstores. It contains a currency converter to help customers easily compare prices. Book search criteria include country of delivery and choice of currency payment.

CNET / http://www.cnet.com. This technology portal features price comparison, product reviews, and technology industry news for computer hardware, software, components, and accessories. It is useful for experts who need to remain current on new technology and for consumers wanting to buy it. It offers free software downloads, which prompts users to return to the site.

Dealtime / http://www.dealtime.com. This site allows users to search for products and compare prices in different online stores ranging from clothes and toys to office equipment and travel. Once customers have selected a product, they are pointed to the seller's site to buy directly. Convenient interactive buying guides, particularly for electronic goods, help users make an informed choice.

Epinions.com / http://www.epinions.com. Consumers can read and submit ratings of products and services in categories from cars and electronics to banking services and travel holidays. The highest and lowest customer-rated products are displayed, helping users to find a bargain or avoid a poor deal. Users receive recommendations on products and advice, and may earn money for sharing their opinions on the site.

IBuyer.net / http://www.ibuuyer.net. Computer hardware and software price comparison site that also features product reviews. Contains links to online stores. Hosts a moderated discussion group for specific products and the industry through which members can exchange information, questions, and answers. A "bargain bin" on the site lists special offers.

Let's Buy It / http://www.letsbuyit.com. Features collective consumer buying or "co-buying," which allows buyers to negotiate lower prices from suppliers through bulk orders. Potential buyers decide whether to join a co-buy and pay the "current price" (whatever price is reached when the co-buy closes) or the "best price only," which may not be reached. If the best price is not reached due to an insufficient number of buyers, "best price" buyers' orders are cancelled. Sites are operating in France, Germany, Sweden, and the UK.

MySimon / http://www.mysimon.com. This product and price comparison site has links to online merchants' sites in France, Germany, and the USA. Seasonal features include back to school items, and some earn special mention as "editor's picks."

Priceline / http://www.priceline.com. This site provides reverse auctions for airline tickets, hotel rooms, rental cars, long distance phone calls, mortgage financing and new cars. The customer names a price and agrees to be bound to it if the offer is accepted. The customer is informed within 15 minutes whether a supplier has accepted the offer. Customers who are flexible with travel dates or the number of airline connections are "rewarded" with cheaper fares. The user submits credit card information with the offer, with the understanding that the credit card will be charged immediately if the offer is accepted, and that the charge cannot later be reversed.

uSwitch.com / http://www.uswitch.com. Compares electricity, gas, and mobile phone services offered by providers in the UK. Consumers select a few service preferences to begin the matching process for the most suitable supplier. USwitch considers the consumer's payment preferences, service expectations, energy usage, location, and cost when suggesting a supplier. Consumers benefit from free and impartial advice about the most suitable supplier.

ZDNet / http://www.zdnet.com. Online shopping magazine features buying guides for technology products. Contains product reviews, a buyer's alert, and links to other Internet shopping magazines. Users can find local content through ZDNet's many international sites.

Consumer-to-Government/C2G Web Sites
REGULATORY AND TAX COMPLIANCE WEB SITES

ATO Assist / http://www.ato.gov.au. The Australian Taxation Office has developed a "user-centered" design to help citizens through their site using intuitive navigation.

Direction des Impots / http://www.mfie.gov.ma/di/index.htm. The Directorate of Taxes of the Kingdom of Morocco allows individual and corporate taxpayers to download tax forms and relevant information circulars.

Gobinet / http://www.barbados.org.bb. The Government of Barbados Information Network (Gobinet) is "positioning itself to serve global information needs and achieve greater transparency in government operations." The portal includes links to ministries and news. It also allows users to link to their own local government, business, regional, and cultural issues.

India Image / http://www.nic.in. The portal site of the government of India links ministries and agencies. The "Citizen Services Gateway" is a link to online telephone directories, passport-applications, downloadable tax forms, national railway schedules, etc.

Inland Revenue / http://www.inlandrevenue.gov.uk/. The site provides news, forms, contacts, and tax information for citizens of the United Kingdom.

Internal Revenue Service / http://www.irs.treas.gov. Allows citizens of the United States to file their taxes electronically, provides answers to frequently asked questions, contact information, and a link to consult with an independent tax ombudsman.

Office of Community Development / http://www.rurdev.usda.gov/locd./. Highlights the successes of the national Empowerment Zones and Enterprise Communities program.

Promudeh / http://www.promudeh.gob.pc/. National program to promote literacy and to prevent domestic violence by the Peruvian Ministry for the Advancement of Women and Human Development.

Republic of Slovenia / http://www.sigov.si. The Ministry of Informatics implements C2G programs and advises about information technology matters for other ministries. The "e-administration" portal covers almost all aspects of e-government including registration of vehicles, driving licenses, births and deaths, foreigner employment, electronic forms, personal identity cards, and other legal forms of identity.

Telecom Egypt / http://www.mcitel.gov.eg. Allows customers to pay their telephone bills online by providing online or telephone assistance.

Consumer-to-Consumer/C2C Web Sites
AUCTION OR ADVOCACY SITES

Association pour le Developpement de l'Internet en Pharmacie Hospitaliere / http://www.adiph.org. This French site for hospital pharmacists is maintained by an association for development of the Internet in the area of hospital pharmacology. The aim is to help members to use the Internet effectively in their work. Provides contact e-mail addresses, calendar of events, and other helpful links.

AuctionTalk / http://www.auctiontalk.com. Encourages online auctions by providing discussion fora, news, and a listing of over 2,700 auction sites searchable by location, product, and name.

Car Today / http://www.cartoday.co.za. An automotive-related portal for consumers in South Africa providing news, sales statistics, and buyer guides. The "autolocator" allows searching through the country's largest database of vehicles for sale.

EBay / http://www.ebay.com. This is a very popular online marketplace for the sale of goods and services by individuals. Buyers search for auctions by category (e.g., consumer goods, concert tickets), region, theme items such as Valentine's Day gifts. It features millions of items for sale by auction and facilitates payment through the Pay Pal micropayment system.

ENTERWeb / http://www.enterWeb.org. Lists and rates other sites that have a focus on enterprise development, business, finance, and international trade. Lists what ENTERWeb finds as the best sites on issues such as finance, education, training, information technology, etc.

GirlGeeks / http://www.girlgeeks.com. Seeks to enhance the careers of professional women in information and communication technology fields by providing training, networking, and information.

Global Museum / http://www.globalmuseum.org. The intent is to provide news, contacts, and advice to museum professionals. Fee-based services include courses on museum management, bookstore, and a free competition for the best museum sites.

Learn the Net / http://www.learnthenet.co.za. This is a free site. It has an easy-to-understand introductory course on the Internet, e-banking, and technology for South Africans. It provides links on the history of the Internet, how to conduct e-commerce, using search engines, how to select an ISP, etc.

Travlang / http://www.travlang.com. Online language center offering free and fee-based language courses, travel guides, foreign language dictionaries, etc.

UDDI / http://www.uddi.org. The Universal Description, Discovery, and Integration of Business for the Web seeks to list buyers and suppliers on the Internet. Also, companies specify their preferred software applications for business transactions, allowing others to find companies with compatible software programs for electronic transactions.

Category Killer Web Sites
OTHER GREAT SITES

About.com / http://www.about.com. Over 700 experts in 20 countries maintain Web pages ranging from aerospace to wireless communications. In addition to thousands of useful links, many subject experts publish regular newsletters in their area of specialization. The site is consistent in format, and a built-in search engine allows for easy navigation.

American Society for Quality / http://www.asq.org. ASQ is a society of individuals and organizations dedicated to the development and promotion of quality concepts, principles, and techniques. A simple site design makes finding answers to questions simple. The site offers a unique e-learning center. Users can submit applications for ASQ certification.

Africaonline / http://www.africaonline.com. This portal site for Africa contains news on current affairs, how to do business, sports, etc. It contains a directory of more than 10,000 Africa-related sites in categories from government to travel and tourism. It hosts discussion fora on a host of issues.

Britannica / http://www.britannica.com. This site provides a vast amount of material from the famous Encyclopaedia Britannica at no charge to users. It contains an online store selling Britannica products such as DVDs, maps, and software. A powerful search engines finds related articles from scores of magazines and links to 125,000 sites.

HotJobs / http://www.hotjobs.com. Over 3,000 registered recruiters review the resumes of more than 300,000 people. No head-hunters are allowed on the site. Users can post information and take part in an online forum to exchange employment tips. Search options enable the user to carry out job searches by keyword, company, job search firm, and location.

Hotmail / http://www.hotmail.com. This free Internet-based e-mail service allows the user to send, receive, and store e-mail messages from anywhere in the world. Available in 12 languages, other services include free newsletters and personalized calendar. A very simple registration process allows novices to open accounts quickly. Accounts are deleted after 30 days of non-use.

Office.com / http://www.office.com. This portal aims to service the operational needs of business people regarding hiring staff, business development, financing, buying business products and office supplies, etc. It hosts an online marketplace for business products, and peers can interact on the site to make contacts, get ideas, share success stories, and have questions answered through online discussion fora.

Telesonique / http://www.telesonique.ch. A telephone company in Switzerland, the firm made a modest investment in Web marketing and virtually zero in advertising. Designed as a sales and customer service tool for customers seeking phone service in Switzerland, the site informs customers about service, prices, and terms. Accepts customer registration through the Internet or by phone.

Webby Awards / http://www.Webbyawards.com. Since 1997, Webby Awards have been given for creativity and use of technology. This site lists all active sites of past winners. If you would like your site evaluated, consult the site for when to submit an entry.

Yahoo!Groups / http://www.groups.yahoo.com. A "group" is a collection of e-mail address and sites of users with shared interests around the world. The site allows groups to form easily by using a template.

With thanks to Prima De Sousa of the International Centre for her research and analysis of many of these sites.

5

The Secrets of Electronic Commerce

Information about the Internet is often confusing, confounding, and contradictory. This chapter is meant to provide practical, simple answers to common questions regarding the Internet. The secrets of e-commerce are not really secret. It is just that you too often will really have to dig or try a variety of approaches before you begin to understand the issues critical to success.

First, though, a brief history of how the Internet came into being will help bring the simplicities and complexities of the Internet into perspective. This history is based on a review of Otis Porter's "How the Net was Born and Where It's Headed" in *Newsweek* (www.businessweeke .com/1999/99_44/b3653086.htm) and *Electronic Commerce and the WTO* (author unknown; WTO reference URL no longer available).

Origins of the Internet

The first electronic communications network was established in 1969, when four universities in the USA, together with the US Department of Defense, developed a network of computers known as ARPANET to allow academics to access remote information using computers. ARPANET enabled researchers to hold online discussions, access offsite databases, exchange electronic files, and send e-mail as early as 1972.

ARPANET's Network Control Protocol, which controlled the way information was sent over its own network, was replaced in the early 1980s by TCP/IP, another protocol. TCP/IP standardized the flow of information across networks and identified users through the use of Internet addresses or domain names. Its main advantage was the uniquely robust way it dealt with messaging, using individually-addressed pages of information. It was designed to provide secure communication during an uncontrollable event such as a telephone line failure or even nuclear attack. Although it was the key to enabling and increasing communication between early computer networks that resulted in the communications network now called the Internet, its limitations grew more and more apparent as the condition that demanded it (unreliability of the network) became less important.

In 1990, Tim Berners-Lee created the Web when he established the first Web site at the European Center for Nuclear Research (CERN), the particle physic laboratory on the France-Switzerland border. Berners-Lee's inventions included hypertext transfer protocol language (HTTP) and uniform resource locator languages, which made it possible to create a vast "web" of documents linked together across a TCP/IP network.

In 1991, the World Wide Web was the exclusive province of NeXT computers, because the hypertext portion exploited a "hole" in the NeXT operating system. After Berners-Lee released his initial software as an open-source code on the Internet in 1991, other NeXT users began to add ideas. The Internet spread the word of Berners-Lee's work, which caused users of other computers to write their own browser programs and applications. The following year, in May, Pei Wei, a student at the University of California at Berkeley, created Viola, a Unix browser that set the early standard for Internet-based graphics. That summer, CERN's Robert Cailiau and Nicola Pellow created a browser for Macintosh computers. In February 1993, a student group at the University of Illinois led by Mark Andreessen introduced Mosaic for IBM-compatible personal computers.

Retail E-Commerce: Its Role as a Model

In the retail e-commerce environment, businesses can conduct more targeted, aggressive marketing at a fraction of the cost of traditional retail advertising, even to a very large customer base. Other retail businesses have created a single site to generate worldwide sales. Once the site's reputation is established, many then branch out to other products.

Retail e-commerce is expected to increase as a sales medium because consumers can benefit from instant price and product comparisons. They can also participate in different pricing mechanisms such as fixed prices, auctions, and reverse auctions. In addition, the great transparency that exists in the pricing of goods and services and the reduced need for traditional middlemen are likely to make prices more competitive.

The retail Internet has weaknesses, although the most pressing appear to be remediable:

- Order fulfillment and delivery are the most important but least efficient aspects of retail e-shopping. However, as more businesses begin to mix online and offline retailing with new automated warehousing and delivery mechanisms, businesses are able to handle delivery more efficiently.
- Not all types of products sell as well as others. E-shopping has so far been more successful with "low-touch" goods, such as computers, books and CDs, which consumers do not need to see and touch, than with "high-touch" goods such as clothes.
- Another widely perceived weakness is the lack of secure payments, and especially fear of the theft of credit card numbers.

So, is retail e-commerce modifying traditional business models? It seems that it is, because the role of business intermediaries is changing. Many types of retailers, for example, are being replaced, as manufacturers can now sell direct to consumers. New intermediaries are being created, including shopping agents and ratings sites, Internet portals that act as shopping malls, and aggregators offering a new way of amassing buying power.

Two major issues surround these new models. The first concerns the competition they bring to traditional intermediaries, whose mark-ups have been large in comparison to their contributions to the value chain. The second has to do with the question of whether the models are on the side of the consumer or of business.

In an article titled "A survey of e-commerce," *The Economist* (February 26, 2000) argues that the best of the new intermediaries will have to act as agents for the consumer. Businesses that sell goods over the Internet have to adapt their distribution systems to a warehouse-cum-truck system (which can deliver a single package to an individual household) or outsource distribution to specialized firms. Although managers of traditional businesses were not slow to realize the potential threat posed by e-commerce, they faced and still face difficulties in adopting new business models quickly. These difficulties seemingly arise from the fact that managers have first to convince those who have invested time, money, and effort in the previous business model: suppliers, employees, bankers, shareholders, even customers—who are therefore likely to resist change.

According to www.nua.com, the E-tailing Group found the average number of clicks to checkout had fortunately decreased since the fourth quarter (Q4) of 2000 from 8.76 to 5.36, and from 4.93 in 2002 to 3.76 in 2003.

Basic Technical Foundations for E-Commerce

E-Mail/Web Connection

An e-mail/Web connection requires a computer system, e-mail addresses, Web connection through an ISP, and a domain name/site. A basic site allows your clients to place orders, submit inquiries via e-mail, and search for information. However, with only a site and Web connection, this system is not connected to information systems that support the operation of the firm (i.e., there is no Enterprise Resource Planning connection).

Enterprise Resource Planning (ERP)

Enterprise resource planning software integrates business processes into information technology. For instance, by using a spreadsheet program such as Excel for purchase orders, an ERP system eliminates duplicate entering of purchase order information because all processes of the company are processed by one integrated system. ERP systems are the central nervous system of an organization, responsible for storing, organizing, and presenting financial, process, and performance information. Software suppliers such as SAP and Oracle have developed enterprise-oriented software systems. More detailed information can be found at http://www.erpassist.com.

Enterprise Resource Planning Software Systems

An ERP system can be built by purchasing software with interfaces for your *existing* software or by programming interfaces between your existing non-compatible software. ERP systems cut costs through automated transfer of data, allow you to "see" the entire firm's electronic operations, reduce chance for human error, and allow you to integrate systems with your customers' systems for a seamless order and production e-commerce cycle.

Application Service Provider (ASP)

An application service provider allows businesses to rent software, including ERP systems modules, instead of having the enterprise purchase it. ASPs also install and service the system, train staff, and provide support and follow-up. An ASP assumes all risks when running, for example, the ERP system, processes the databases of your company using their equipment and software, and assumes responsibility for electronic transactions, Web hosting, system development, etc. Therefore, it is unnecessary to hire IT staff. Using an ASP allows you to use integrated software systems without paying high up-front costs of having, for example, an ERP in-house.

Software and Hardware Needed to Go "E"

Hardware

The hardware requirements for e-business are simply a computer with the latest memory capacities and computing power standards. Opting for computers with older standards will inevitably result in having problems when installing and/or implementing new software.

Software

Buying appropriate software can be more complicated. Following is a checklist of some basic software you will need to become ready for e-commerce. Some software may be directly downloaded at no charge from the Internet.

Browser Software

Browser software allows you access the Internet. The most widely used are Netscape Navigator or Microsoft's Internet Explorer.

E-Mail Software

E-mail software allows you to send and receive electronic messages and attachments. Popular brands include Eudora, Groupwise, or Microsoft's Outlook.

Office Software

Office software package such as Microsoft Office often includes compatible software packages such as word processing, spreadsheet calculating, an Internet browser, an e-mail program, and a slide-show presentation software such as PowerPoint.

Virus Scan Software

When your computer is connected to the Internet, you will be exposed to contamination by external viruses. Virus scan software such as Norton or McAfee is essential to prevent potential losses of information and damaged software, which could be costly in terms of recovery and repair. To guard against potential virus attacks and/or theft, you should also frequently back up your business documents and data by copying them onto external disks and storing them in a safe place off-site.

Application Servers

To access data, run server pages, and manage sites, an application server will be needed.

Commerce Platform

In order to run an e-commerce application, a commerce platform will be needed.

E-Commerce Application

E-commerce applications allow for order placing and purchasing using the Internet.

Content Management

Businesses will need to share certain information with suppliers, customers, and employees to maintain documents, fulfill orders, process payments, and integrate documents with internal employees and external buyers and suppliers.

Customer Service Applications

How businesses provide customer service is increasingly the most important factor when differentiating an online business.

Enterprise Portal Server

Enterprise portal servers provide employees self-service access to administration functions such as performance and project planning reports, expense tracking, and other internal company data and documents.

Integration Servers

Integration servers blend external buyer and internal systems together.

Customer Service/Marketing Automation Application Servers

Automated software allows businesses to respond to customer inquiries without human intervention.

Types of Internet Connections

Internet service providers (ISPs) install a connection from your computer to the Internet, and can supply e-mail addresses and a company's URL (site address). Maximum waiting time for downloading Web pages at peak traffic times is affected by the type of connection used ranging from slow analog telephone modem connections or faster ISDN, DSL, cable lines or wireless connections. Slow connections can affect the time and accuracy of downloading software, sending and receiving attachments, video streaming, etc.

Choosing, Registering, or Buying a Domain Name

Your domain name is key to your strategy, because that is where your customers will find you. Among your alternatives for a domain name would be your company name, the name of your top product line (brand name), an acronym. The name should be what most of your customers know you by or how you want them to know you. Be careful of acronyms—they may be too obscure. You may want to pick both your first and second choices, in case your first choice has already been taken.

Either have your ISP obtain a domain name (the name of your site) for you for a fee or register it yourself with the appointed registrar of your chosen top-level domain (TLD) and then get your ISP to do the rest.

Which TLD should you be in? For a business, is it better to be in the .com domain than in a country-code domain? In principle, you can register domains in almost any of the top-level domains except .mil (reserved for the military), .gov (reserved for governments), .int (reserved for certain international organizations), .org (reserved for certain not-for-profit organizations), and .edu for educational institutions.

The best domain to be in is the one where your users are most likely to look for you. This may be the .com TLD. But that TLD is now very crowded, in the sense that it is increasingly difficult to find an appropriate domain name that has not already been registered. Also, many of your users may be accustomed to adding the country code TLD (such as ar, my, and za for Argentina, Malaysia, and South Africa, respectively) to the names of the hosts they are seeking. If you do not use the country code of the country where you are located, you will make it more difficult for local users to find you. Some of the most effective search engines and directories are regional search engines: they are frequently more thorough in indexing or listing sites within a region than the global search engines.

You can find out who the appropriate registrar for your chosen domain is—and how to contact them—by asking your ISP or by checking with the global registrar of registrars at whois.htm. You can register (buy) a domain name from a registration group such as Internic at http://www.internic.net, or other name specialists such as NetNames at http://netnames.com or Register.com at http://www.register.com. You will need to tell the group what your ISP's address is. As mentioned before, you can buy a domain name directly from your ISP, although it will charge extra for this service.

You can register a domain name (for example, mycompany.com) without actually being on the Internet. Registering a domain name is similar to registering a company name in most countries: the name must meet certain criteria (such as uniqueness). A domain name must be unique within any TLD because duplication could lead to confusion and possible misrepresentation. Many companies register their domain names as soon as they can (some do this even before their host computers are linked to the Internet) to ensure that no one else can take their chosen name. A registration fee is usually paid.

If you want to associate a domain name with a host computer linked to the Internet (frequently the host name of a computer that provides a World Wide Web server is simply "www"), you need to obtain a numerical Internet address and to arrange for that address to be notified to other computers on the Internet. Again, it is usually easier to have your ISP do this for you because the notification procedure requires that at least two servers maintaining domain names on the Internet must know about the link between your domain name and the numerical Internet address of your host computer.

A computer with a unique Internet domain name and number does not need to be permanently connected to the Internet. The system will not break down if a host cannot be reached because the owner is not linked via a dial-up modem, for example. However, users will become impatient and lose interest if they find a "host not reachable" message when they try to connect.

Keep in mind also that national or regional search engines will only index sites with a domain name from the region they are intended to serve. For example, a business in Brazil may have to register as my-company.com.br, and not mycompany.com, in order to be registered by a regional search engine as a site in Brazil.

E-Mail Address Options for Business

E-Mail Addresses with an Internet Service Provider Domain Name

An ISP provides e-mail addresses with their own "domain name." For example, if you select Internet services from the GTX Internet Service Provider, your e-mail address may be something like: yourname@GTX.com. An e-mail software package such as Eudora, GroupWise, or Outlook serves as a "user interface" to your e-mail for sending, receiving, storing, and replying to messages.

E-Mail Addresses with Your Domain Name

Unlike e-mail addresses supplied by ISPs, these addresses will reflect your company's domain name. Your "Web space" provider will assign a Web page address for your company and e-mail addresses reflecting that home page. Therefore, an e-mail address for an employee at ABC Company could be: Mr.Wujjoh@ABCCompany.com.

Web-Based E-Mail Account

A Web-based e-mail account allows you to bypass using an ISP. Instead of receiving e-mail messages using an ISP account and checking them via your e-mail software, messages are received on an Internet site using your business address. For example, ABC Company can create an e-mail account with Yahoo. The e-mail address would be Mr.Wujjoh@ ABCCompany.com. Using Web-based accounts are helpful when traveling, in countries with a limited number of ISPs, or when you do not want to engage the services of an ISP.

Obtaining a Web Site Address

A site address is given through an Internet Protocol (IP) number. A "domain name" for that number is then registered through the Internet Corporation for Assigned Names and Numbers (ICANN). You, an ISP, or "Web space" provider can register the domain name and "host" your Internet site. You will need to decide whether you want to store your site with the ISP, or if you will install a Web server in order to update the site by your system whenever changes are made. Either way, registering will effectively connect your company domain name to your IP number.

You can directly register your site with ICANN's licensed registration service called InterNIC (http://www.InterNIC.com). Registering allows you to obtain a domain name license which lasts for two years and costs approximately US$70. InterNIC's site contains a list, indexed by country, of accredited Web space providers.

Establishing a Web Site

Establishing a site requires obtaining Internet access, obtaining Web space, and developing a site. The cost of developing a site varies by country and by the business or individual developing it. Average costs to develop a site are generally based on an hourly fee and the size of the site: the larger the number of pages and technological features, the higher the fee. Therefore, it is important to plan your site architecture, text, and photos, and make the fewest possible changes once the process has begun.

Marketplaces Online

E-marketplaces match buyers and suppliers. A 2000 Forrester Research survey of more than 500 corporate leaders said that 71 percent plan to extend their internal business processes to e-marketplaces by 2001. By 2004, more than half of the US$2.7 trillion worth of B2B trade conducted online will take place in electronic marketplaces. E-marketplaces are listed in the Retail Systems Alert at http://www.retailsystems.com. Samples of online electronic marketplaces include:

http://www.mbendi.co.za	African-Produced Products
http://www.e-markets.com	Agricultural Products
http://www.globalcoal.com	Coal
http://www.netbuy.com	Electronic Parts

http://www.chemconnect.com	Chemicals and Plastics
http://www.wiznet.com	Electronic Filing and Content Repository Software
http://www.metalsite.net	Metal Industry
http://www.pulpandpaper.net/	Paper Industry
http://www.tradeport.org	Information on Marketplaces by Industry

Once you find marketplaces that interest you, compare registration fees, services, and regions covered by the marketplace. Typical services of an e-marketplace include:

Auctions and reverse auctions
Buy–Sell offers
Buyer requirements/supplier capabilities
Calendar of events
Catalog of products with photos and technical specifications
Directory of companies in the industry
Directory of companies by product name
Equipment for sale
Evaluations by portal users
Financial services
Freight transportation management/customs management
Import regulations
Industry forecasts
Industry news
Industry reports
Investment news and stock indices
Links
Market prices
Newsletters
Order tracking system
Preferred supplier lists
Pricing information
Production guidelines
Quality standards
Ranking, "testimonials," or comments from suppliers on buyers

Auctions: Buy- and Supply-Side

When posting goods on a marketplace, you reach a wider range of potential customers rather than by posting goods only on your site and promoting your site.

- *Buy-Side Auctions (where buyers list their needs):*
AuctionBiz	http://www.auctionbiz.com
Egghead	http://www.egghead.com
FairAuction	http://www.fairauction.com
Sorcity	http://www.sorcity.com

- *Supply-Side Auctions (where sellers list their offers):*
Excess Inventory	http://www.tradeout.com
Used Equipment	http://www.imark.com
Shipping	http://www.gocargo.com

Reports and Trade Publications

Often easily found by typing targeted key words into a search engine, highly-focused industry reports, analyst reports, and trade publication articles have been developed for hundreds of business sectors. Typical sites include:

http://www.argusonline.com	Oil and Gas Sector
http://www.argribusinessonline	Agricultural Products
http://www.manufacturing.net	Manufacturing Processes
http://www.plasticsnews.com	Plastics

Finding Information about Your Competition

The most important primary sources of information on what your competition is doing are trade journals on your area of business. Journals usually provide updates of the state of the market (domestic and/or international) for your product or service, as well as company news, analyses, and profiles. Two examples of industry trade journals are:

- *Metal Bulletin.* Deals with the metal industry; published twice weekly; has a site at http://www.metalbulletin.com/.
- *The Grocer.* Covers the food and drink industry in the United

Kingdom; published fortnightly; has a site at http://www.
foodanddrink.co.uk.

Reference databases list primary sources of information that have been
analyzed and indexed, making it much easier to find specific information through the use of search keywords.

Some examples of pay-to-use online databases are listed below. These
are provided by DIALOG'S DataStarWeb, DIALOG Corporation, Palace
House, 3 Cathedral Street, London SE1 9DE, United Kingdom.
http://support.dialog.com/products.

- PTSP—Gale Group PROMT® Plus. Searching through the database is charged by the second, and the cost per hour is US$90,
  and the average download cost is US$2.50. PTSP is a multi-
  industry database with abstracted information on companies,
  products and markets. http://ds.datastapweb.com/ds/products/
  datastar/sheets/ptsp.htm.
- INDY—Trade & Industry Database. Searching through the database is charged by the second, the cost per hour is US$90 and
  the average download cost is US$3.17. INDY is a full-text data-
  base with information on companies, products, marketing
  and other subjects. htttp://ds.datastarWeb.com/ds/products/
  datastar/sheets/indy.htm.
- Reuters Business Briefing Search—Available at http://www.
  factiva.com. Subscription fees are charged in local currencies;
  US$approximations are: US$750 per 20-hour block, US$450 for
  the first 10-hour block and US$375 for each additional 10-hour
  block. The database contains research reports from worldwide
  authorities in marketing, economic forecasting, company profiles and investment analysis. Reports are available on a pay-per-
  view basis.

  Note: Business periodicals such as the *Financial Times* (published daily) and *The Economist* (published weekly) also contain
  company and market information. Their respective sites are
  http://www.ft.com and http://www.economist.com.
- *CIA World Fact Book* by the US Central Intelligence Agency—
  Available free at http://www.odci.gov/cia/publications/factbook.
  html. Also available in print (US$92; non-US, US$128).
  Superintendent of Documents, PO Box 371954, Pittsburgh, PA
  15250-7954, USA. Tel: + 1 202 512 1800, Fax: + 1 202 512 2250,

E-mail: gpoaccess@gpo.gov. Provides political, geographical and infrastructural information, as well as economic indicators on individual countries.

- *Country Commercial Guides* by the US State Department—Available free at http://www.state.gov/business. Superintendent of Documents, P.O. Box 371954, Pittsburgh, PA 15250-7954, USA. Tel: + 1 202 512 1800, Fax: + 1 202 5 12 2250, E-mail: gpoaccess@gpo.gov. The guides provide a "comprehensive look at countries' commercial environments, using economic, political and market analysis."

- *Economist Intelligence Unit's Country Reports*—US$450 per year for four issues per country per year. For Europe, the Middle East and Africa, contact Charlie Segal, The Economist Intelligence Unit, 15 Regent Street, London SW 1 Y 4 LR, UK, Tel: +44 20 7830 1007, Fax: +44 20 7830 1023, E-mail: Lndon@eiu.com. For Asia and Australasia, contact Amy Ha, The Economist Intelligence Unit, 25/17 Dah Sing Financial Center, 108 Gloucester Road, Wanchai, Hong Kong, Tel: +852 2802 7288, Fax: +852 2802 7638, E-mail: hongkong@eiu.com. For the Americas contact Albert Capozelli, The Economist Intelligence Unit, 11 1 W. 57th Street, New York, NY 10019, USA, Tel: +1 212 554 0600, Fax: + 1 212 586 0248, E-mail: newyork@eiu.com. Provide information on each country's business development, economic and political trends, etc.

- *Exporters' Encyclopaedia*—Dun and Bradstreet, One Diamond Hill Road, Murray Hill, NJ 07974 - 1218, USA, Tel: + 1 908 665 5000, Fax: + 1 908 665 5000. Subscription and sales: Tel: 1 800 526 065, E-mail: customerservice@dnb.com. Update inquiries: Tel: + 1 6 10 882 7000. Hotline for export questions: The Americas, South-East Asia and the Pacific: Tel: + 1 610 882 6124; Europe and North and Central Asia: Tel: + 1 610 882 6376; Africa and the Middle East: Tel: + 1 610 882 7260. Information on trade regulations, documentation requirements, transportation and legislation affecting commerce in over 220 countries.

- National Trade Data Bank—US$75 per month for a CD or online subscription. US Department of Commerce, Washington, DC. 20230, USA. Tel: + 1 202 482 1986, Fax: + 1 202 482 2164, E-mail: stat-usa@doc.gov. More than 20,000 full-text worldwide industry/country and market studies conducted by US Trade Counselors abroad.

Product and Service Factors That Sell

Use of Unique Terms to Describe the Product or Service

If your product or service can be characterized or described in unique terms, it will fare better on the Internet because it will be easier to find through search engines. Be sure to refer to your product or service with the combination of terms that searchers are likely to use when looking for your type of product, as well as to ensure that these terms appear with sufficient frequency on the Web pages that you have asked your search engines to index.

Competitive Pricing

Because the Internet helps customers to compare prices for identical goods, the identical goods priced the lowest will sell the most. Also, for all products, online prices may have to be lower than in-store prices in order to create an incentive to overcome the consumers' lack of trust in online retailers. This is partly due to the absence of an interpersonal exchange in the transaction, as well as to compensate for the customers' inability to "take the product with them."

The Touch Factor

Consumers continue to want to touch, see, smell, try, "kick," or talk to someone about a product before they buy it. Some sellers may still need to make their products available at retail outlets or other physical settings where consumers can "touch" them before they return to the Internet to make the purchase.

Uniformity of Product

Manufactured and mass-produced goods are easier to sell online than hand-made or custom-produced items. Manufactured goods are more consistent in their characteristics, have predictable production costs, and are generally better known to consumers. If customized products are available, set up a contact link for direct communication with the company.

Non-Immediate Needs

Consumers are more likely to order non-urgent consumables online, rather than goods they need immediately. Manufacturers that are able to work to pre-set production, shipping and delivery schedules, are also more likely to use the Internet for their procurement purposes.

Consumer Understanding of the Product

B2B commerce on the Internet will increase faster than consumer purchases from e-commerce firms (with the exception of the largest of these firms, such as Amazon, Autobytel, CD Now, and Dell). This is because, unlike many consumers, businesses are familiar with the specifications of the products they need and are therefore more comfortable with ordering on the Net.

Regularly Purchased Products

Standardized products purchased on a regular basis (e.g., groceries, standard clothing items, office supplies, books, etc.) are familiar to consumers and therefore easier for them to purchase over the Internet. Buyers feel that such purchasing saves them time and relieves them of some of the boredom of repetitive shopping.

Services That Sell Well on the Internet

The success of a services business on the Internet depends on some of the same things that make any business successful, such as the degree to which the products of the business meet a market need and can be produced profitably.

However, services businesses are particularly suited to the Internet because their products tend to be produced or delivered with digital information processes. Most services businesses involve the collection, storage, manipulation, and dissemination of information. Some examples are:

- Accounting
- Advertising
- Auction services
- Commercial education and training
- Computer services and software
- Customs brokering
- Education
- Engineering

- Financial services
- Health (telehealth) Insurance
- Industry news
- Management consulting
- Market research
- Personnel search
- Print and graphic design services
- Site design and maintenance
- Travel and tourism
- Writing services of all kinds (freelance journalism, technical writing, editing, etc.)

A quick search through a major Web directory site such as Yahoo (www.yahoo.com) or Google (www.google.com) can easily turn up many more examples of categories of services being supplied across the Web.

Products That Sell Well on the Internet

It is predicted that the major growth sectors in e-commerce will be the global media and entertainment industry, tourism (hotels and airlines), professional and financial services, insurance, and retailing. Research has shown that product-specific success factors include having a strong brand, selling a unique product and offering competitive prices online.

It should be noted that not enough research has been conducted on e-consumer psychology to determine why particular segments of consumers or businesses purchase products and services and why they do not do so.

An interesting question is the extent to which it is possible to change the purchasing behaviors of consumers and businesses. Perhaps it is easier for businesses to change than to reduce costs, improve delivery time, communicate with suppliers, and simply to attain efficiencies in ordering, shipment and delivery. Furthermore, perhaps the incidence of B2B purchasing is higher because it is so distinctly unlike a traditional personal shopping experience. We must question whether it is not in the consumers' nature to want to wander around the big bazaars, the shops in local town centers, the malls, grocery stores, or whether they would prefer to shop online in order to spend more time on pursuits like sports or with the family.

Finding Buyers

Among the sites that list prospective buyers are:

- European Business Directory, at http://www.eurapages.com. The site displays over 500,000 companies from 36 countries and is freely accessible.
- Kompass International Database, at http://www2.kompass.com. Probably the largest source of company profiles, the site has detailed product classifications. It covers 1.5 million companies in 60 countries and 23 million products.
- WLW online, at http://www.wlw.de/com. The site covers more than 240,000 potential suppliers in 10 countries in various European languages.
- World Trade Center Association, at http://www.wtca.org/. With 300 center-members in 180 countries, WTCA offers a directory of 140,000 importers, exporters and related businesses.

Getting Products Listed Prominently by Major Search Engines

Obviously, it is in your best interest that your site is easily found. According to some sources as many as 85 percent of Internet users find sites through search engines. With more than 4,000 sites being added each day, any enterprise selling or promoting its products on the Internet must make sure that these products are listed with the search engines in the way that its prospective customers will find it.

A typical search engine looks for matches to words and phrases in a large index that it compiles from Web pages found on the public Internet. The search engine uses software known as a "spider" (or "robot") because it is configured to follow the links in the Web from one page to another, usually one site at a time, much like a spider following the threads in its web.

The best way to improve the effectiveness of searches for your site is to practice using differing key words or sets of words. Use search engines frequently, experiment with different types of key word and natural language searches, ones that your prospective customers would most likely use. Experiment with several search engines to get a feel for the scope of each, as well as for the user interface that you prefer.

Because the Web has an enormous text content, search engines are often very selective about the depth to which they will index a site and the amount of text on any page that they will attempt to index. Most search engines work with sites' meta tags—those key words used by your company and the industry or profession in which you are working—in order to come up with the right Web addresses when an Internet user conducts a search for information. A few search engines ignore meta tags, and some engines use other factors to determine what to index on a page.

Regardless of the methods that search engines use, the content to which they pay the most attention is usually a combination of the text within the "Key words" and "Description" meta tags on a page, the page title or the words in the first few hundred characters of a page. Not all of these items are important to every search engine. To make your company easily found on the Internet, you need to decide on the key words of your site. If they are not already in your materials, these key words should be inserted on the main page of your site.

No matter how search engines index a Web page, they all respond to a user query in similar ways. They draw from their index database a ranked listing of pages whose entry in the index matches the search terms entered by the user. The rank of any site in this list of search results reflects the exactness of the match, according to criteria established by the search engine programmers.

This is why it pays to think carefully about the terms that your users are likely to enter into a search query when looking for your products (or your competitors' products). You must ensure that your pages give prominence to those terms in the areas such as the page title, meta tags, and the content of the top text that the spider robots are most likely to select for indexing. The more closely your content reflects the phrasing of the most popular queries, the more likely it is that your site—if it has been indexed by the search engine—will be listed near the top of the results found by the user's query. Keep in mind that a search for a popular item such as "tennis" will find more than one million sites.

You should also be aware that intentionally and unnecessarily repeating meta tags in the content of a Web page in order to try to increase your chances of getting a hit, known as spamdexing, has a negative effect on a site's ranking with most search engines.

How can you ensure that your page will be indexed by a particular search engine? Most indexing search engines allow you to "register" a URL that will be added to the "to do" list of the search spider. You can register your site with search engines via e-mail, sending your site's name and key words directly to the search engine. Look for a link such as "Add a URL" somewhere on the search engine page. Follow the link and carefully follow the instructions given. Most engines require you to enter a URL and an e-mail address. You do not need to enter a separate address for all the pages on your site. In most cases, the spider will follow links on your site from one page to the next, although sometimes only to a predetermined depth. Also, some spiders are not very good at handling links through a frameset (the portion of the pages that is framed).

For helpful tips on how to register your pages—and links to some free registration helpers—see, for example, www.searchenginewatch.com. The Web page at www.searchenginewatch.com/webmasters/article.php/2167931 provides help on using meta tags.

To be listed among the top ten sites, you should use site submission services, such as www.submit-it.com, www.netcreations.com, or http://we.register.it. They have specialized knowledge of how search engines prioritize meta tags and, for a fee, they will tailor meta tags for your Web pages. Check these sites for price quotes and for a list of the other services offered.

The Leading Search Engines, 2005

Google	http://www.google.com
Yahoo	http://www.yahoo.com
Ask Jeeves	http://www.askjeeves.com
AllTheWeb.com	http://www.alltheweb.com
AOL Search	http://aolsearch.aol.com (internal)
	http://search.aol.com/(external)
Hot Bot	http://www.hotbot.coin
Teoma	http://www.teoma.com
AltaVista	http://www.altavista.com
Gigablast	http://www.gigablast.com
LookSmart	http://www.looksmart.com
Lycos	http://www.lycos.com
MSN Search	http://search.msn.com
Netscape Search	http://search.netscape.com
Open Directory	http://dmoz.org/

Internet Directories. An Internet directory is compiled manually (i.e., with human involvement), which implies that a directory is likely to be more selective than search engines. One of the best known Internet directories is Yahoo! You should check how much it costs to be registered with, and listed on, directories. You need to apply to a directory to have your site listed.

Start with a large search engine within your targeted region. If you can't find a large search engine specific to the region you want to search, try using a generic large search engine, and typing your region of choice as one of the key words.

E-Mails: Writing Them Effectively*

While e-mails have become important to personal relationships, they are an important component of e-commerce as well. We all know that the greatest advantages of e-mail are savings in time and cost. Everyone uses e-mail for informal communications: to send memoranda, notices, reports and newsletters; and to post offers to buy and sell, etc. And we all know that the amount of e-mail we receive on an annual basis is increasing. According to Global Resource Group, in 2000 the average business manager making US$75,000 a year in the United States received and sent an average of 74 e-mail messages a day; in 2001 the average was 127. And according to Pitney Bowes, in the United Kingdom an average of 27 e-mail messages were sent and received in 1999, up to 39 in 2000, with an exponential increase of 191 in 2001. Unfortunately statistics are not available for later years, but we could just all look in our In and Out message boxes to see the increasing numbers of messages that are processed each day!

With the significant increase in the number of e-mail messages, the following are ways for you, as a manager, to craft a succinct, to-the-point message:

- In the *To:* line, type in the e-mail address of the intended recipient.
- The *CC:* or "carbon copy" (from the days when sheets of carbon paper were interleafed with regular paper in order to make identical copies) line allows you to send a copy of your message to other persons to keep them informed and to secretaries responsible for the electronic filing of messages.
- *BCC:* stands for "blind carbon copy." This feature allows you send a copy of your message to another person without letting the

*This section is co-authored by Natalie Domeisen, International Trade Centre (Geneva, Switzerland) and Sarah McCue.

addressee in the To: or CC: line know that you have done so. For mass mailings, use the BCC feature to address each recipient so that he or she will not have to scroll through a long list of addresses in the To: or CC: lines. Moreover, by using the BCC feature, you will keep your list a secret from others. By preventing others from seeing your list you will also reduce the amount of spam mail that could be sent to your customers.

- In the *Subject:* line, be brief, use active verbs and provide key details of your message. Many readers decide whether to read a message on the basis of the subject line alone. If your messages are mislabeled, you not only waste your readers' time, but you also take the chance of failing to communicate your point. If you can put the most important point of your message in just a few words—no more than four or five words—on the subject line, your e-mail will be more effective. For example, a message with the subject "Time of staff meeting," or "Invitation to staff meeting" misses an opportunity to save every one the trouble of opening and reading the message. If, instead, the subject had been "Staff meeting, 2:00 pm, Thursday," everyone would have understood the message immediately. The details of the venue and who should come are probably less important—because everyone may know them anyway—and can be put in the body of the message.

- Be careful to review those subject lines when you are using the automatic "Reply" feature, i.e., the lines that begin "Re: Re: Re: Staff meeting". By the time the message has bounced back and forth a few times, the subject of the exchange at this point is usually quite different from the original message. Always change the subject line to convey the current message. In place of "Re: Re: Re: . . . ," the subject line could read "Sending electronic handouts before meeting."

- When sending e-mail, send copies only to those who need to see your message. Consider carefully whether you need to send business associates a copy of your message. What you may consider an effort to communicate may be regarded by others as of no interest or value. Instead of deluging your manager with "just wanted to keep you informed" types of e-mails, you should consider what many firms are requiring: that managers provide only a weekly update of their activities which summarizes all those e-mail messages, actions, and decisions made.

- Be sure to give your name, title, address, telephone and fax numbers (with your country code), and e-mail address in all correspondence. You may want to create an automatic signature for insertion at the end of each message so that you do not have to type this information each time you send a message.
- Make sure your message is clear. Do you have ambiguous or confusing language that may be misinterpreted? Have you spelled out acronyms (unless you are *sure* the recipient understands them). Have you checked for spelling and grammar mistakes?
- Be on your guard against too much informality or frankness in e-mail messages. Although e-mail is a quick-and-easy, casual medium much like conversation, most people find it much harder to convey their meaning as accurately in writing as they can in person. If your reader cannot see the smile on your face, he or she may be offended by your use of words. Your offhand remarks, too, will probably hit home more sharply in writing than in person and seem more like genuine anger or wounding sarcasm. It is a good rule to be consciously "mellow" in e-mail. Once you have pressed the send button, you cannot take back your words or soften them in an afterthought.
- If you need your reader to act on something mentioned in the e-mail, state it in the beginning. If you are communicating with more than one person, address each paragraph to a particular person. For example, you may want to instruct Mr Ahuja to handle a particular task in one paragraph, and Ms Aruba to handle another task in the next paragraph.
- Reply promptly to messages, usually within 24 hours. Use the "Automatic Response" feature when you are away, so that senders know when to expect you back or whom to contact during your absence.
- Do not type out words in capital letters. This is the equivalent of shouting.
- In addition to e-mail, many businesses have turned to real-time methods of communicating over the Internet. Use of Internet relay chat (IRC) and voice over Internet protocol (VOIP) applications allow businesses to interact with customers instantly. Many service providers offer these applications free of charge. Among these providers are AOL, HumanClick, LivePerson, and

Yahoo. Internet relay chat is a system for real-time discussions over the Internet; the discussions are carried out on "channels" devoted to specific subjects. VOIP uses the Internet as a transmission medium for telephone calls.

News Groups, Listserves, and Direct Marketing

News Groups

Usenet news groups are public international news groups that allow participants to discuss issues related to a particular product, service, issue, or interest. News groups are generally open to all and can be run at low cost using widely available—often free—software from an Internet server. Private news groups managed on your own server or hosted by one of the many low-cost hosting services can be an effective way of building up your enterprise as a source of expert information. Many online businesses use private news groups as a forum for customers to exchange information, helpful hints, or complain.

Listserves

These are electronic lists of individuals stored in an e-mail system who receive group or mass communication via e-mail on a regular basis. You can make your own list on your computer by entering e-mail addresses into a database or an address book. A listserve is a low-cost or no-cost means for providing instant information and updates to a group of individuals who seek information on a particular product, service, issue, or interest.

Listserves may be moderated (screened for content) or un-moderated. They may distribute digests (summaries of messages compiled according to themes) rather than individual e-mails. (See also "News Groups" and "Direct Marketing.")

Direct Marketing

E-mail addresses can be used to promote your services, advertise coming events, or solicit new customers. Lists of these addresses can be an inexpensive source of reaching large numbers of target customers, especially for a mass market approach. Because so many online businesses have overused this method, however, most of us have an instant negative reaction to receiving e-mail messages from an unknown source.

Commercial Lists. Some e-mail lists currently being sold for direct marketing purposes are random collections of e-mail addresses that are poorly maintained. They contain addresses, which, if genuine, are frequently those of persons who have not asked to be added to the list and who do not welcome the large number of irrelevant offers, unwelcome opinions, and even offensive material that they receive. It is wiser to create your own lists and not use lists from these list providers. If you must purchase an existing e-mail list, at least purchase one prepared by a reputable marketing company.

Discussion Forum or Virtual Conference: Organizing an Effective, Well-Attended Event

Many businesses use discussion groups (un-moderated or moderated) and virtual conferences as a way to keep customers informed, engaged, and connected.

Discussion Forum

Un-moderated discussion groups are similar to conference telephone calls or group meetings where participants are free to interject comments throughout the meeting with no moderator. Often participants will ask the virtual group a question to which various members reply to the whole group. Others use the virtual group to post invitations, announcements and news of interest to all, or for the joint development of an agenda for a live meeting. Each submission may vary from two lines to a page, and attachments may be included.

Moderated discussion groups are similar to seminars, and last from one day to a span of several weeks. Most use moderated discussions to share experiences on a particular issue, to facilitate business-related networking, and to explore customer needs. With these types of discussions, it is important to choose an effective moderator who is familiar with the topic; comfortable with stimulating interaction electronically; and able to provide a concise introduction, midway summary, and a conclusion reflecting the group's discussion.

Virtual Conference

Virtual conferences enable people from around the world to participate with little or no travel costs. Such conferences help develop common positions, lead to an understanding of client needs, stimulate networking, sharing of information and concerns and encourage the participation of individuals who may not feel comfortable speaking at a live conference. Often virtual conferences are used for developing and promoting joint strategies, disseminating best practices, fostering bilateral contacts, and providing a collective venue for product or project announcements.

Because they are resource-intensive (though far less so than a live event), full-fledged virtual conferences are not held too often. People frequently assume that Internet events require little resources other than technical support platforms. As the points below indicate, conference management, promotion, contents and strategic development are required for virtual conferences as much as for live ones. In addition, organizers need to work with participants to create the appropriate conference tone and etiquette, and to ensure that suitable technical support is available.

Organizing Steps

Develop an Interesting Agenda. Determine the key issues you want to discuss and how the information gathered will be used once the event is over.

Create a Sense of Expectation. Develop and post a conference agenda, so that participants can anticipate contributions of special interest to them. Conduct an official opening and closing of the conference.

Find Good People to Manage It. Holding a discussion or conference involves someone to promote the event, gather e-mail lists, set the agenda, moderate, edit, and organize the contributions, and technically support the event.

Don't Leave Conference Interaction to Chance. Before the event, line up a moderator, conference "speakers," and individuals who will provide "comments from the audience." As with moderated discussion groups, strong moderators, strong commentators, and a wide base of participants are essential.

Get High-profile Contributors and Moderators. Line up high-profile keynote "speakers." Create an advisory board, the members of which should contribute presenters, moderators and/or discussants on behalf of their organizations. Identify the events (live or virtual) which have recently taken place on the same theme, and then ask their organizers to make a presentation in your forum on the recommendations or best practices that emerged from those events. Carefully plan the sequence of presentations from speakers, so that the group can move smoothly towards conference conclusions.

Promote the Conference Creatively. Write an announcement and request related sites to post it. Ask these sites to create a link to your conference site (if available). Send out very short e-mail announcements to hundreds of targeted participants. Line up luncheons, office visits, telephone calls or electronic advance meetings with key speakers and moderators. Encourage all of them to send the conference announcement to their staff, sites, or magazines.

Promote Early and Everywhere. It is best to promote the discussion or conference at least one month prior to the event. Use conferences, flyers, magazine articles, e-mail announcements, links to related sites, telephone calls, faxes, visits to organizations, meetings. The more high-profile the event, and the higher the expectations in terms of strategic results, the greater the investment is required in promotion.

Establish Conference Etiquette.

- Train participants to make concise and readable presentations, so that the information given can be easily assimilated by busy professionals.
- Ensure that keynote speakers limit their contributions to one to three pages. Comments on discussions should not exceed one page.
- Discourage "airbag" comments and encourage substantive ones.
- Encourage participants to send comments directly to the person concerned and not necessarily to the entire group.
- Put contact information at the beginning or end of each contribution (whether from a speaker, discussant, or moderator), including the name of the person concerned, his or her organization, title, and e-mail address, to facilitate the type of networking that occurs in live conferences.
- People may be interested in announcements on new projects or products, but this information must be inserted properly or participants will feel they are being made a target for advertisements.

- Keep a record of the presentations and discussions in archives on a site for use by researchers and organizers after the event.

Improved Communication through E-Mail and Web Sites

The long-term success of any business or organization is built on relationships. Listserves, online surveys and newsletters, and virtual discussion groups and conferences can help build such relationships. However, to obtain more mileage from these activities, carry out what is called customer profiling or customer relationship management (i.e., building a data file on every client, interacting with clients on a one-to-one basis or within groups of like-minded individuals). You could also supply clients with information on a need-to-know basis by using targeted e-mail lists.

Despite its universal use, even mis-use, e-mail remains a widely used, but little understood communication tool that can provide instant, free, targeted messages to existing and potential customers, employees, managers and suppliers, and colleagues in the industry and industry professionals. Some ways of targeting communications to these different groups are set out below.

Communicating with Customers. Send regular e-mail updates to customers, letting them know of sales, new products, or company developments. Only one percent to two percent of those who visit a site buy anything, while 90 percent of those who enter a physical store buy something. Much of the disparity in the buy rate has to do with customer service. E-commerce companies need to address the problem of providing exceptional "red carpet" online customer service. Good customer service ensures contact with a real person who will solve problems, respond quickly and well to all inquiries, and follow up after a purchase. Automated responses to customer inquiries are strongly discouraged.

Communicating with Managers. Many e-mail messages to senior staff members (e.g., those concerned with finance) could also be sent to others in the marketing, production departments, etc., so that all key management staff are kept up-to-date on company matters.

Communicating with Employees. Circulate among your employees new and updated information. This could include news about your company's overall sales performance, its new customers, employee contributions, new employees, new ideas, minutes of senior staff meetings, employee manuals, training documents, etc.

Communicating with Suppliers. Suppliers should be given regular updates on shipping and delivery needs, production and supply schedules, etc.

Communicating with Colleagues and Professionals in Kindred Professions. Establishing a moderated listserve gives professionals within a particular industry the opportunity to share views, industry developments and concerns.

The following are some ways to improve communication and customer service through e-mail and sites:

- Appoint someone to manage client relations through communication, customer services and information dissemination.
- Add clients' e-mails to your database and create a segmented listserve. Differentiate your clients on the basis of their needs.
- Get clients to talk to you by using online surveys, listserves, and moderated discussion groups.
- Create a weekly or monthly e-mail newsletter.
- Have direct Web links to every customer's site.
- Conduct regular electronic surveys and send your customers the results. Include an "aging" system that will tell you when your customer has last contacted you. Have the system alert you when x days have passed, so that you can follow up.
- Use video-conferencing as a low-cost way of interacting with your clients.
- Archive reports online, with related topical links.

Providing Secure Payment Systems
Credit Cards

When designing your site for payment transactions, make sure that it is secure for these transactions to protect both you and your customer. Credit card sytems will involve using the secure electronic transaction (SET) payment-card protocol. Advanced by Visa and Mastercard, SET provides confidentiality of payment and order information, ensures the integrity of transmitted data, authenticates the identities of cardholders and merchants, and allows for the reversal of transactions if this should be necessary.

Authentication and Encryption Services (Digital Signatures)

You will also need authentication and encryption services. Authentication validates identity or proves the integrity of information. In public key systems, authentication requires the use of digital signatures. Encryption converts information into a form unintelligible to all except holders of a specific cryptographic key. It protects information between the encryption process and the decryption process (the inverse of encryption) against unauthorized disclosure.

> AdvantageMerchantServices.com
> AllianceData.com
> Cardservice.com
> Charge.com
> CyberCash.com
> Cybersource.com
> Ifsab.com
> ITransact.com
> Verisign.com

Choosing an Internet Service Provider and Web Site Designer

Given the explosion in the number of Internet service providers (ISPs) and Web designers, select them carefully. Telephone companies, cable TV operators, specialized business-only providers, schools and governments all offer access to the Internet, and many offer Web design services.

ISPs and Web designers offer five types of services: access through dial-in or dedicated leased lines, site hosting services, site development, specialized Web design services for such features as databases, and Internet training. Here are some questions to ask when discussing your project:

Questions to ask regarding Internet access include:
- Do you offer a flat-fee service?
- How many hours of access can I get each month within the basic fee structure?
- How many users can I add for each line without additional charges?

- Is a free site included in the basic subscription fee?
- Do you offer 24-hour technical support?
- How long is the average wait to speak to a real person at your company?
- When I travel will I be able to have local dial-in access?
- Do I receive free Internet browser software with my subscription?
- How fast is your e-mail delivery?

Questions to ask an ISP hosting a site include:
- How fast is the Internet connection (pipe)?
- How does this compare with the speed provided by other ISPs?
- How much space do I get on the server?
- How much would additional space cost?
- Can I obtain a domain name through you?
- If so, what does it cost?
- What site management tools do you offer?
- Do you provide a server log-analysis tool to show me details of the use of the site?
- Do you offer Telnet and FTP access to the site?
- Do you have restrictions on CGI programs running on the server?
- Do you offer value-added services such as Microsoft FrontPage extensions?
- How fast have you grown and what is your growth plan?

Questions to ask site designers include:
- How many sites have you developed for a fee?
- What are the addresses of the best sites you have designed?
- What are the least and most expensive sites you have created?
- Who does your graphic design?
- How will graphics be used in my site?
- Can you reduce the size of images?
- Have you worked for my competitors?
- How will you help us publicize our site?
- Will you register our site with (regional, global, specialized) search engines?
- What is included in this service?
- Do you charge for changes to be made to the site?
- How long have you been creating sites?

The following are key steps to take when creating a Web site:

- Decide on the information you want to convey and the transactions you want to achieve.
- Determine who will use your site.
- Discuss how you want to organize the information to ensure that you communicate your message clearly.
- Organize the materials and information you want to have on your site—its architecture. Create a chart with branches, and headings and subheadings, so that viewers can quickly find the information needed and not waste time going through information and documents that are not relevant to their search. Start to outline the site on paper in general terms, i.e., develop a storyboard for it.
- Select key words to use strategically on your site for the search engines to index.
- Collect images for the site from an electronic library or CD-ROM. These can be pictures of products, your building, key staff. They can also be icons, clip art, or graphics that convey concepts and ideas.
- Transfer the images onto the computer with the aid of an image scanner, and change or alter them with a graphics program to suit your sizing and color needs.
- When you have your outline, you will be ready to create the site using the basic hypertext mark-up language (HTML). Convert your written text to HTML, which can be done in Dreamweaver, Netscape, Homesite, and several other HTML editing packages. There are a number of user-friendly software programs that will convert electronic texts into HTML without your needing to know anything about HTML.
- Find an Internet service provider (ISP) to host the completed site.
- Register a domain name.
- Register your site with search engines.
- Promote your site among your target audience.
- Monitor the search engine(s) you choose, to ensure that your site is and continues to be listed prominently. With having a prominent listing a strong part of your strategy, expect to spend three to four hours a week on this in the beginning. Once you reach the level that you can in these areas, expect to spend an additional two to three hours every month to work on the site.
- Update the content of the site regularly.

Secured Servers:
How to Set Them up Cost Effectively

This section describes a complete system. A smaller enterprise may not require all the elements covered and may find it easier to ask its Internet service provider to establish the secure server.

A "secured" server implements network and physical security measures, such as a firewall and physical access controls, to protect a server using any electronic transfer mechanism such as the Internet Protocol, ethernet, or any other network system. You must distinguish between a "secured" server (defined above) and a "secure" server. The latter is an HTTP server that uses digital signatures (certificates) and a secure sockets layer (SSL) protocol (or its descendant protocols) to identify the server host and possibly the client host, and to encrypt communication between them.

There are two ways of hosting a secured server: through an ISP or onsite, administered by the enterprise itself. Hosting at an ISP can be less expensive in terms of training, equipment, and telecommunications costs. However, by outsourcing this function, the enterprise is dependent on the service, security, and responsiveness of the provider.

When establishing a secured server within an enterprise, there are two aspects to consider and both are important. First, the server must be physically located in a limited-access area open only to authorized staff. Second, the Internet security system should be behind a firewall that has been professionally installed and configured. A firewall has three interfaces: the external, which is seen by the outside world; the internal, which is partially seen by the outside world; and the trusted, which is invisible to the outside world.

The physical system can be split into two separate parts for added security. The part of the database containing the most confidential material (credit card numbers, accounts, etc.) is held on the trusted interface of the firewall (the interface that is not accessible from outside the network). The area with which the user interfaces is held on the internal interface, which is partially seen by the outside world.

In terms of hardware, you need a dedicated telecommunications line connected to the Internet in order to allow your clients to access your site. The line must be large enough to carry data quickly. It should be upgradeable. A firewall system will be needed as well. There are many types of firewall systems available and at various price levels, from US$1,000 to US$20,000. Comparison pricing is advisable. A good system is the WatchGuard firebox, easy to install and robust, available for around US$4,000.

Promoting Your Site: Generating More Leads

All too often businesses do not promote the site through links and other means, whether online or offline. Attracting prospective customers to your site does not necessarily require additional funds for marketing, but it will take effort and time. Some ways of generating more traffic to your site are for you to:

- Register key words of your site with multiple Internet search engines.
- E-mail customers the address of your new site, allowing them to click on your site instantly upon receipt of your announcement.
- Establish links to sites that are related to your industry, but not in competition with you.
- Write articles describing sites of interest to your industry and include links to your site.
- Print your site and e-mail addresses on stationery, business cards, labels, brochures—all the places where your street address appears.
- Notify sales representatives how to use the site and how to promote it to new customers.
- Offer discounts to customers who order online.
- Send eye-catching or humorous postcards about the site.
- Set up distribution lists of client groups for e-mail marketing.
- Send e-mail newsletters or industry updates once a month, and include your site address.

6

Trends in E-Commerce

In defense of the founders of thousands of Internet start-up firms in the late 1990s who thought they could create a profitable business shipping, for example, discount dog food from Maine to California—and the investors who believed them—e-commerce was an untested sales and marketing medium. Technology specialists, Web designers, and newly graduated MBAs with not much business experience formed a new vision for a new e-conomy. Despite their inexperience and untested business models, millions upon millions of dollars were poured into e-commerce start-ups by equally inexperienced and blind angel investors and venture capitalists.

Many assumptions were made, including the now ridiculed "banner advertising strategy" in which Web site revenue came only from advertising. However, the strategy was largely ignored by users who were not charged for using a site.

Another model rejected by consumers was the offer of free goods or information in exchange for personal information. This type of "glee-commerce" mentality was just not logical and soon faded as a sustainable business model. Then "fee-commerce" made a brief foray, as digital cash was thought to be a viable way to charge users for the sites they visited. And yet this model failed because of concerns about security and overall reluctance to pay small micropayment amounts per click for Internet-based information.

Soon B2B e-commerce became the darling of the e-commerce world because it was thought this is where "real" businesses would buy from and supply each other from around the globe through the use of online ordering, payment, customer service, and other integrated software systems. The problem is that B2B e-commerce requires intra- and inter-company integrated systems using shared software and databases, sharing of valuable and once hoarded information among colleagues and between firms, and exposing systems, policies, processes, procedures, and prices not only to internal staff and clients, but also to competitors.

Horizontal and vertical management information systems, common software, and overall management practices of the business between buyers and suppliers need to be integrated and systematized into one seamless, faceless, automated Internet-based transaction.

Unfortunately, only the most visionary, professionally managed, strongly led, and team-oriented businesses are able to achieve this state of efficiency and effectiveness. Creating B2B systems is much like achieving ISO9000 status. The process is often painful but results in a more open, sharing, efficient, and automated environment. But for many firms, the human, financial, and organizational impact is often too great. That is why B2B e-commerce has not infiltrated the procurement world as deeply and widely as expected.

Next, came "we-commerce," wherein like-minded firms within an industry gather into one global marketplace where buyers can find the best deal from hundreds of firms posting their offers. The industry portals offer auctions, buy-sell offers, calendars of trade shows, company directories, equipment sales, financial services, industry forecasts, market prices, order tracking systems, wholesale prices, and shipping management services . . . just a few of the services offered at this one-stop shop on the e-commerce superhighway. This may sound too good to be true, and, for most portals, it is. There are few portals that effectively and consistently offer these services because the industry and the businesses that comprise them are not organized yet for portal-commerce.

Industries Changed Most Profoundly by E-Commerce

What industries have been—and will be—changed most profoundly by e-commerce? Just about all of them.

The six industries that have been changed most profoundly by e-commerce, thus far are computing and electronics, telecommunications, financial services, retailing, energy, and travel.

Computing and Electronics

Together, Dell Computers, Cisco Systems, and Intel sell more than US$100 million a day over the Internet. For most makers of personal computers (PCs), however, the Internet continues to present a dilemma:

whether to cede online sales to direct sellers like Dell and Gateway, or risk alienating retailers by selling online and thus "cannibalizing" their own distribution chains.

Telecommunications

Because of the burgeoning use of data transmission through e-mail, servers and millions of sites, revenues from telecom services to businesses are expanding for global leaders.

Financial Services

Financial services are easily digitized, deliverable online, and inexpensive. In 2003 it cost banks in the United States only US$0.01 to process an Internet-based consumer transaction, compared with US$1.07 for a branch and US$0.27 for an ATM transaction. Although growth is fast, there have been concerns expressed that complex regulations and security concerns are stifling competition and growth.

Retailing

Thousands of sites have been created by traditional retailers, thus offering many thousands of goods direct to consumers.

Energy

Led by online sales of natural gas, trading in other energy such as electricity, coal and fuel, is also taking place online because of the ability to respond immediately to rapidly fluctuating demand. It is predicted that most transactions will veer from existing brokers to online exchanges, such as Altra Energy and HoustonStreet.com, breaking down traditional geographic boundaries, spurring competition and lowering prices.

Travel

Millions of consumers have bypassed travel agents to book tickets and other travel arrangements online, significantly reducing their costs. It costs just one dollar to process an e-ticket compared with eight dollars for an agent-booked ticket. According to ClickZ Stats, in 2005, 70 percent of consumers with online access book air travel online with online travel booking sites, such as Expedia, Orbitz, or Travelocity versus 25 percent who call an airline's service directly. And 81 percent of respondents said price is the single most important factor in their decision on which site to book a flight. Ease of use was the second most important factor, identified by 50 percent of respondents. (Rob McGinn, "Online Travel Companies Edge Airline Web Sites" Mar. 3, 2005; http://www.clickz.com/stats//sectors/travel/article.php/3487426.)

Changing the Way Business Is Conducted

The greatest and most obvious trend is that the Internet and technology will continue to redefine the way we live, learn, love, communicate, co-operate, work, and play.

We are in a unique position to benefit greatly from the Internet and technology. We can also be hurt by it. On one hand, technology will continue to redefine people's jobs, giving them more autonomy, flexibility, information, and responsibility, all of which have the potential for greater impact, efficiency, and effectiveness. On the other hand, manual laborers used to create what a machine now can, middlemen used to sell a manufacturer's products to customers within a designated region, and women used to do tasks in offices with their hands that machines now can. These are just a few examples of how technology can help through improved efficiency—and hurt because people are losing their jobs.

Certainly the Internet and technology are powerful forces that can propel the economies of all countries if properly understood. If not, un-defined, vague, and yet angry protests will continue to occur as they did in Seattle in 1998 at the annual meeting of the World Trade Organization (WTO); the International Monetary Fund (IMF) meeting in 1999, Prague; the Doha/WTO meeting in 2001; and the World Economic Forum meeting in 2000. And, very much related, the mas-sacre of innocent business men and women working at the World Trade Center on 11 September 2001.

The cold reality is that faceless businesses, eager technologists, and the people who believe in global commerce will continue their quest for success without much thought to the people who are shouting that their lives, cultures, and incomes are being gravely affected. Some suggest that perhaps many of the protestors should spend less time shouting than accepting the reality that the global economic landscape is being redefined and that there is not much that can be done to stop it. However, with this acceptance comes the obligation of training in, un-derstanding of, and using and benefiting from technology to ensure that both cultures and economies survive—and thrive. To do so, we must understand the trends that are affecting our lives and livelihoods, so that other, more subtle trends can help our world, not hinder it.

Corporate Responsibility

Increasingly, companies are being rated not only on profit-making ability but also on their responsibility as good "corporate citizens." For example, the Dow Jones Sustainability Index rates companies on what is known as the triple bottom line: economic criteria (e.g., innovation, branding, margin); environmental performance (ecologically sound manufacturing processes); and social awareness (human rights, lifelong learning, children's educational programs, volunteering).

Time and again, e-commerce and information and communications technology companies will be asked if they are partnering with firms in developing countries to educate, expand access to Internet, and create "sister" relationships much like the "sister city" concept wherein cities forge long-term social, educational, and humanitarian relationships with cities in developing countries.

The Partnering Firm

Being a responsible firm is not only the ability to respond to the need to do good and more in developing countries. It is in the best interest of all businesses if strategic alliances, partnerships, and joint ventures are formed not only within the country but also in countries where its citizens survive on less than two dollars a day.

Government agencies, businesses, educators, universities, and non-profit organizations that attempt to create more partnerships, strategic alliances, and joint ventures with entities in these countries will have dug far into the mine when others realize the only place for real growth is in countries that have not experienced growth for decades.

Democratization

Perhaps the most undeniable trend of all is that developing countries sooner than later will create democratic institutions, universities and training institutes, and viable pro-business infrastructure in the form of satellite infrastructure, drinkable water, roads, and other basic needs of civilization. Once this happens—and it is happening now—firms that have already shown themselves to be caring citizens will find it much easier to penetrate these diamond mines of economic growth and development.

Profound political changes are occurring before our eyes. Scores of countries have joined the World Trade Organization and agreed to take the "bitter medicine" of standardization, transparency, and liberalization, and to disconnect life support systems from its agricultural and other protected industries. Privatization of telecommunications and other industries has occurred in scores of countries, thus contributing to lower prices and greater competition. These are just a few examples of how the world is becoming a more open and competitive place, which creates confidence in a country. This, in turn, is followed by investment, new businesses, and the creation of a middle class increasingly able to improve its standard of living.

Make no mistake. Just as the Industrial Revolution was triggered by Watt's improvement in the steam engine in the mid 1770s, the creation of a railway system in 1829, a pre-paid postal service in the 1830s, two world wars in the first half of the 20th century, mass computerization in the late 1980s, and commercialization of the Internet in the 1990s, democratization of the world in the early decades of the 21st Century will be the latest, greatest, and most profound change to affect the world economy.

Focus on Aging Populations

In every single developed country, but also in China and Brazil, the birth rate is now well below the replacement rate of 2.2 live births per woman of reproductive age.

As the population around the world shrinks and large cohorts such as the Baby Boomers in the United States become older and focused more on leisure and lifestyle conveniences, e-commerce companies will do well to respond to their needs.

For example, online advertising will focus more on explaining to older people the benefits in time saved through online shopping, convenience of home delivery of such products as water, groceries, and furniture. Creating family-focused sites that emphasize "keeping in touch in touchless times" will make the Internet seem less lonely to those without direct human contact—important to older individuals whose family may be located sometimes in five different countries in three different time zones.

Multilingual Sites

English will likely remain the *lingua franca* of the Internet. But firms that respond to the linguistic needs of their customers will be leaders in the marketplace. With instant and online translation programs becoming increasing accurate and essentially free, there is less reason why a site cannot be fully informational and transactional in multiple languages. Make sure your Web designer provides a multilingual site, even though the designer might not like maintaining dual- or multilingual sites because changing one small page means changing it for the other sites as well. Software that is linked to the mother page is increasingly adept at simultaneously changing all languages at one time.

Shift to Nontraditional Labor

With technology and pervasive access to the internet, it is increasingly easy for people to work any time, any place, replacing the typical 9 a.m. to 5 p.m., stay in your cubicle traditional job. More and more people will work as temporaries, part time staff, and consultants for multiple firms that outsource marketing recruitment, sales, customer service and back office functions.

Increasingly, firms will rely more on project assignments than on traditional jobs based on the "strategic vision" of a boss with 20 direct reports. Savvy e-commerce businesses will realize that people are motivated whether or not managers can see them in their offices everyday. Thus, they will allow for outsourcing of employment in other countries, or allow individuals to work out of their homes and still be in constant contact with the office through instant messaging, video phones and computers, ability to send and receive large attachements, etc.

Management of people will have less to do with managing personalities in the work place and more to do with managing resources to retain motivated employees who prefer to work anytime, any place.

The downside of having a cadre of employees who do not have a desk, office/cubicle, telephone and chair in a designated space at the firm is that individuals may feel less connected or loyal to the employer and, thus, move more easily from firm to firm.

The flexible firm that creates ways to keep the employee connected, motivated, and focused will be the firm most sought by perspective employees.

Continuing Education

It is almost too obvious to point out that constantly changing software, their applications, and ways of living and working differently require all of us to embark on a lifelong quest to stay informed, relevant, and competitive. Online training, subscriptions to electronic newsletters, newspapers and journals, and participation in electronic discussion groups are but a few of the ways that we will keep ourselves informed on very specific areas of interest.

For example, an individual might subscribe to the InfoDev electronic mailing list to keep informed about what developing countries are doing to bridge the digital divide; CNN news lists for breaking political and economic developments; Forrester, NUA, and Information Weekly for weekly updates on electronic commerce research, news and developments; a listserve for the latest programs developed in international trade; and an electronic newsletter for cooks. Add to that subscriptions to the *International Journal of Electronic Commerce, The Economist, TIME, Discover, Choices*—a UN quarterly magazine—*National Geographic*, and *Bon Apetit*. Add to that maybe an average of 50 e-mail messages a day and making or getting 10 telephone calls per day. That same person might watch CNN in the morning prior to work, listen to news radio on the way into and out of work, and catch the evening news. This information-gathering lifestyle is typical of most working-age professionals and describes the author's information sources. Of course, most of us risk the threat of information implosion where nothing gets read and an increasing general sense of angst as the information received does not get processed. This is why it is mandatory that firms of the future focus on not only knowledge gathering or acquisition but management of it.

Focus on Knowledge Acquisition and Knowledge Management

We have all heard the term *knowledge management* but what does it mean for 21st-century business practice? As knowledge becomes instant, free, and focused, firms that attempt to harness the vast supply of information will be victors in the marketplace. Now more than ever, information is power but how can firms empower individuals to create power and opportunities from information?

First, internally, employees should be encouraged to spend at least an hour a day reading all that input they are receiving, including online newsletters, participating in discussion groups, and surfing the Internet for the latest developments in a particular industry. Many receive daily or weekly industry news updates but are too overburdened with "processing" their work, that they do not have time or motivation to keep themselves informed.

Another key trend will be management's strong encouragement of employees to share information with each other. For example, traditional weekly staff meetings are "what I'm working on" kinds of meetings but will be transformed into "what I learned" meetings to identify trends, developments, and overall strategic direction.

Also, firms will increasingly take the time to identify the informational needs of customers and then respond to these needs by offering focused, short, and targeted information via e-mail, on its sites, and other paperless and stampless means of communicating with customers.

Communities of Customers

Increasingly, "communities of customers" will be developed so that individuals in a particular community (e.g., online billing) can interact with, learn from, and develop, refine and share technology with each other. Software standardization and inter-operability is increasingly important. Therefore, informational barriers and protection of company secrets will be less important as communities of like-minded people share successes, discoveries, and challenges.

For example, there is a magazine titled *Billing* for telecommunications companies who bill their companies online. Instead of providing a one-way flow of information via the magazine informing readers of new developments, increasingly these groups will form their own online discussion groups, chat rooms, and instant messaging to learn from each other.

The point is not to give away strategic information that would be detrimental to the business, but for communities of individuals (e.g., specialists, customers, employees, developers, managers, etc.) to interact more frequently than at costly annual meeting conferences or by gaining knowledge through static means such as magazines.

Online Customer Service

"Your call is important to us. Someone will be with you within 5 minutes" was the mantra of the 1990s, when voice mail took hold. Auto-responding to an e-mail that says "Thank you for your e-mail. Someone will respond within an hour" will be the manta of the 2000 decade.

Customer service will become increasingly important as more and more companies realize that creating an effective site does not allow the firm to ignore the customer.

How many times has it been impossible to receive an e-mail response to a query posted online? Even when a company offers discounts to purchase products and services online, the potential customer either seeks the help of a competitor or abandons the quest for information or a particular product because help wasn't available when it was needed—because there was no online or instant customer support.

Currently companies are caught between wanting to save costs by conducting business online yet they are not internally structured to provide online customer service. Companies that use modern technology to respond to customers' need for information and assistance will be part of a growing "we'll get it to you *now*" hyper customer-focused mentality that just is not yet been part of the e-commerce economy.

"Now and Wow" Information Processing and Customer Services

Providing not only online, ontime customer service, but doing the work for your customer will be increasingly common. Firms that respond to the individual customer's preferences whether in terms of custom-made products, targeted information mining and its analysis, or providing tailor-made services will witness repeat customers through their ability to provide "now and wow" customer service.

For example, instead of employment agencies' providing lists of hundreds of job opportunities—now available thanks to the searching and cataloguing capabilities of sites—they are actually applying for these jobs on behalf of the client through a simple matching software. Another example of saving a customer time and money—the real "now and wow"—is a businesses that not only selects and delivers groceries within an hour of ordering, but puts them away—and gives recipes based on the food purchased and knowledge of their grocery inventory. Other examples abound, but firms that not only provide information but also help customers process, analyze, and use the information will be able to provide even more responsive customer service.

In addition, firms will increasingly hire researchers and analysts to mine the information available to them, to create a more efficient, knowledgeable, and effective workforce that is not spending untold and often unproductive hours sifting through reams of information presented to them.

Shifts in Marketing Messages to Explain Better How Internet Services Can Save Time

Despite the potential benefits, many businesses and buyers around the globe are not using the Internet and related technologies as a new way of doing business.

Many consumers do not use the Internet because they do not understand how it can save them time. For example, many do not use online grocery shopping services because the service has not been adequately explained to them. Online grocers have not explained the cost of travel, selection, and loading time (often an entire Saturday afternoon for someone) that can be saved using online grocery shopping. The same can be said for buying clothing, ordering eye glasses, buying, wrapping, and delivering and sending gifts, paying bills online, etc.

Examples of how time and money can be saved using the Internet for services is endless, but promotional messages have not focused much on the "time is money and value" factor. Most advertising messages have been focused on establishing brand identity, not on the inherent value of the product or service.

Change in Organizational Structure

Changing the ways employees "fit" within an organization will have the greatest impact on the growth and development of e-commerce, whether it is for business, government, associations or education. Scary for some and liberating for others, the fact is that technology and e-commerce will continue to affect profoundly the internal organization of firms and other organizations. (See Chapter 3.)

Of course, firms organize themselves in many different ways but the one constant is that technology will change hierarchy. Companies that maintain the traditional, hierarchical organization chart without adjusting it to take advantage of the new electronic economy and technologies will see one or more consequences. One, they will remain uncompetitive due to lost opportunities. Two, they will become frustrated because some employees are attempting to use technology to create efficiencies in their jobs, which is not "part of the job description" or the overall strategic direction. Three, they will be increasingly "turf-focused" as the smarter employees eye technology as a way to improve personal effectiveness, save time, generate more clients, or expand into areas outside of their job description.

For example, consider the manager of communications for a company. Prior to technology, this person would "simply" create news releases; network using the phone, lunches, or conferences; and create paper-based communication tools such as magazines, newsletters, and mailed documents. Now this person is collecting hundreds if not thousands of e-mail addresses of clients and contacts from key employees within the firm; creating virtually no-cost targeted communications e-mail campaigns using hundreds instead of few self-generated contacts; and interacting with internal technology specialists to ensure fast, reliable, and secure systems. What was once a "manageable" position has blossomed into an unbounded opportunity to communicate internally and externally, and easily zoom messages to targeted constituencies. No longer are paper, printing, postage, telephone, and other costs as prohibitive for the communications department. Therefore, most savvy communications people begin to assume a greater role within the corporation by being able to use the Internet, e-mail, CD-ROM, and other means of communication. Some of you may be thinking, "Great! The company is expanding its marketing and communication ability using low-cost technology."

The same is true for Web designers who are increasingly valuable throughout the entire firm as people realize the efficiency, effectiveness, and growth opportunities the Internet can offer them. More and more heads of divisions and individuals within them are attempting to develop their own sites for their own division to communicate with their distinct communities in their own style. What happens in many firms is that there may be a home page that illustrates the corporation as a whole, but sub-layers within the site show an inconsistent theme, little interactivity among divisions, and differing styles. Many firms are attempting to hold tight reins over the content of their site, which results in the increasing importance for the Web designer to integrate various divisions' software, client interaction, database management, customer service, billing, and human resources needs into one cohesive Web site. Hence, what was once perceived as a low-level position should now be viewed as an important and strategic position worthy of a senior management position.

Also recognize the evolution of the traditional secretary's role. The sheer power of technology has irrevocably and forcibly changed the way secretaries do their jobs. Most no longer type memos, copy, distribute, or file them, nor do they answer the phone, send faxes, arrange meetings, travel schedules, etc., because managers are doing it themselves. Correspondence is typed, instantaneously distributed by the person responsible for communicating with clients and is easily filed electronically by the creator of the document. Voicemail allows individuals to leave long messages directly to the person involved. Faxes are rarely sent anymore. Meetings are arranged by quickly and electronically viewing when a space is available for a meeting. Travel is arranged by simply going online. They now create PowerPoint presentations, maintain databases of key e-mail contacts, and participate in meetings as administrative assistants rather than "smiling workhorses" who used to keep everyone organized. Now that many of us are organizing ourselves through such devices as Palm Pilots, instant messaging, cell phones with SMS technology that is a craze in Europe but not at all in the US, electronic calendaring, electronic files, and have the ability to communicate with customers any time and any place, secretaries have become administrative assistants and knowledge managers in the true sense of the word.

And the shift in organizational structure will continue. Exhibit 6.1 shows how employment is slowly shifting from lesser skilled, manual, or administrative positions to those that are more focused on professional, technical, marketing, and services. These are just a few examples of how workplace positions, responsibilities, prestige, and influence will continue to adjust. This will result in some workers increasing their position, responsibility, and influence while others will lose influence or struggle to evolve in response to changing times. Think about how the jobs in your company have changed in the past ten years. Think about who has increased and decreased responsibility. Who is rewarded and why? How did they achieve their success? What makes them more efficient, effective, and successful? In each of these answers, technology has

---

EXHIBIT 6.1 Percentage Distribution of Total Employment in the United States by Occupation

---

Occupation	1988	1998	2008
Managerial	10.3	10.5	10.7
Professional	12.5	14.1	15.6
Technicians	3.2	3.5	3.8
Sales and Marketing	10.3	10.9	11.0
Administrative Support	18.5	17.4	16.6
Services	15.5	16.0	16.4
Agriculture	3.5	3.2	2.8
Production and Repair	11.9	11.1	10.5
Laborers	14.2	13.2	12.7

Source: US Bureau of Labor Statistics.

certainly played a role in their evolution and adaptation to the electronic marketplace and technology-driven firm.

The reality is that nontraditional positions have increased in importance, visibility, and impact. This creates tension throughout most firms due to the need to maintain equality in position and hoard information, which is nearly impossible anymore. There is also the age-old bottom line: professional jealously.

Growing Need for Integration of Systems and Transparency of Information

Software will create more integrated, flexible, and transparent companies but it will also cause tension and fear in the workplace. Linking together disparate computer systems within the firm will result in instantaneous information flow, reduction in information hoarding, and allow employees to understand the "big picture." Having access to information will create efficiencies for the firm, but this information exposure will be threatening to the individual. Think about how often departments build their own systems so they are not reliant on another division, can create a system tailored to their needs and withhold information from coworkers. Most of us remain leery of sharing our information with others in the firm because exposing your information to another is thought to result in loss of power, influence, and autonomy associated with information hoarding.

The truly innovative company will require that all information (except confidential personnel records) be available to all within the firm through organized, logical, and easily accessible electronic filing systems. Certainly some will use this new-found information to their advantage and others will argue that "their" files should not be on public display, but most will use the information to fill in gaps, understand who does what, and create opportunities by being more fully informed.

Prying open the firm will result in initial protests of violations of privacy and the human desire to withhold information, but later most will admit that integrated information access and flow reduces hierarchies, removes departmental boundaries, and creates more team-oriented and collegial employees.

Trends in E-Commerce: Supplier Opportunities and Customer Benefits

Forrester Research found that companies did US$43 billion in B2B electronic transactions in 1998, US$67 billion in 2000. The figure is expected to rise to US$1.3 trillion in 2003, accounting for 9.4 percent of all B2B sales. B2C sales remain small in comparison to traditional B2C commerce. What's behind these figures?

Global Presence/Global Choice

Increasingly, what is happening is that boundaries of commerce are no longer defined by geography or national borders. Because the most important networks are global in scope, electronic commerce enables even the smallest suppliers to achieve a global presence and to conduct business worldwide. The corresponding customer benefit is global choice: customers can select from all potential suppliers of a required product or service, regardless of their geographical location.

Improved Competitiveness/Quality of Service

E-commerce enables suppliers to improve competitiveness by becoming "closer to the customer." Many companies employ ICT to offer improved levels of pre-and post-sales support, with increased levels of product information, guidance on product use, and rapid response to customer queries. The corresponding customer benefit is improved quality of service. And the firm benefits from a more loyal customer base.

Mass Customization/Personalized Products and Services

With electronic interaction using ICT, suppliers gather information on the needs of each customer and tailor products and services to those individual needs. One simple example is an online magazine that can be tailored for the individual reader wherein topics of past interest are emphasized while articles that have already been read will be deleted.

Shortened or Eradicated Supply Chains/ Rapid Response to Needs

E-commerce allows traditional supply chains to be shortened. Using ICT and e-commerce, goods are shipped directly from the manufacturer to the end consumer, bypassing the wholesaler's warehouse, retailer's warehouse, and retail outlet. Since "cutting out the middleman" could be achieved using paper catalogs and telephone or postal ordering, e-commerce simply reduces cost and time. Extreme examples of "squeezing out the middleman" happen when products and services can be delivered electronically, thus altering the supply chain entirely. This has massive implications for film, video, music, magazines, software, and newspapers industries. The corresponding customer benefit is the ability to obtain rapidly the precise product without being limited to those currently in stock at local suppliers.

Substantial Cost Savings/Substantial Price Reductions. ICT and e-commerce significantly reduce transaction costs. While the cost of a business transaction that entails human interaction might be measured in dollars, the cost of conducting a similar transaction electronically might be a few cents or less. Hence, any process involving "routine or mindless" interactions between people offers the potential for substantial cost savings, which can, in turn, be translated into substantial price reductions for customers or increased profitability for the enterprise.

Novel Business Opportunities/New Products and Services. In addition to redefining existing products and services, ICT and e-commerce allow for new products and services such as network supply and support services, directory services, matching buyers and suppliers, and many kinds of online information services.

Global Information Transparency

Buyers can now more easily compare prices and services from suppliers anywhere in the world. Also, quality, delivery schedules, product content, or components can be found on the Internet much more easily than before, thus creating a much more transparent global market.

Mass Customization

Customers can more easily specify individual requirements online, permitting customization of products such as cars, jewelry, CDs, and equipment. Because of lower search costs, customers who enter markets infrequently are now potentially as well-informed about supply and prices as regular suppliers to these markets.

Targeted Communication and Promotion

Incentives can be tailored to individuals more effectively than through traditional marketing media such as television, catalogs, newspaper and magazine advertising, and mass mail.

Global Bidding via Auctions

Auctions, buyers' cooperatives, and barter sites have emerged, with buyers grouping together to obtain quantity discounts. Buyers are bidding on an unprecedented variety of goods through, for example, http://www.ebay.com, http://www.freemarket.com, http://www.priceline.com, and http://www.e-steel.com.

Using Customer Data for Personalized Sales

On the basis of data collected online from existing customers regarding product preferences, purchasing histories, etc., online merchants can offer complementary products to customers by cross-selling or up-selling at low cost and even do it automatically. Economic potential is now more closely linked to the ability to control and manipulate information into commercial transaction.

Earlier Adoption of Discoveries

The Internet will spread innovations much more quickly than in the past. In the 1980s, for example, it took an average of 10 years for an innovation in one country to be adopted in another.

Cut Costs, Not Trees

The Internet will continue to cut costs. A 2001 study by Giga Information Group, Inc., predicted that global savings through business use of e-commerce rather than paper will rise from US $17 billion in 1998 to US $1.25 trillion in 2002. Similar kinds of savings are expected to continue.

The Need to Create Value

Hasso Plattner, the co-chairman and CEO of SAP, the world's second-largest application-software supplier after Microsoft, aptly described how to survive and thrive in the electronic economy. He said:

> In the old New Economy, it seemed that all a company needed to succeed was a URL and a marketing budget. But in the new New Economy, companies are measured by the value they create. Can you increase productivity? Reduce costs? Discover new businesses? (http://www.timeeurope. com/digital—URL no longer active.)

This is the crux of the matter, as companies attempt to develop e-commerce strategies. How will the Internet and its related operations, manufacturing, accounting, sales, marketing, and customer service technology make firms more efficient, cost effective, and bring on new customers? Larger firms understood this in the late 1990s. The trend will be toward smaller companies using similar technologies as well.

Adoption of EDI-Like Software by Smaller Firms

Electronic Data Intechange (EDI) is of only limited value to larger firms if smaller firms are not adopting technology compatible with that of larger firms. Therefore, in the early 2000s, larger firms will begin to demand that smaller firms use the same technology platforms, software, and systems in order to integrate massive and deeply interconnected purchasing systems within the supply chain.

Industry-Specific Portals

Industry-specific portals emerged in 1999 and 2000 as a way to find a one-stop source for information and assistance on a particular industry more easily. Portals at the private and government levels are now seeking to create online, anytime, single electronic access points for customers, clients, and citizens seeking information and assistance. Increasingly, portals will offer the ability for users to conduct business online as well by offering many types of services. Examples include:

- Online licensing and permitting.
- Online filing and secure online payments.
- Scheduling reminders.
- Database integration among sometimes thousands of systems.
- Online counseling and communication.
- Online and interactive training.
- Creation of a profiler and personalization system, static information including simple guides.
- FAQs.
- E-mail information alerts directing the user back to the portal for important updates.
- Discussion forums.
- And many other, limited only by the imagination.

Impact of Wireless Technology

Having Internet connectivity on one's mobile phone is a trend that many are eagerly anticipating; others just aren't that interested. Technologies such as WAP/XHTL, Java, and Multimedia Messaging Service (MMS) and W/CDMA (a global standard for wireless Internet access) keep evolving. Buyers everywhere will be able to use their phones as a personal organizer, surf the Internet at high speeds, play games, or send e-mail with data and photos or short single messages from phone to phone (SSMs). While 200 billion SSM messages were transmitted over GSM networks in 2002, it is clear that people will increasingly rely on their mobile telephone to talk, search for information, send data, and stay in touch.

We will also see larger and larger phones to accommodate bigger and clearer screens with accompanying keyboards as the phone and computer morph into one. The question is, what will it look like, how much will it weigh, how will we carry it, and will form win over function? Will consumers' desire for small gadgets to carry around limit the extent to which the phone will be used as a major contributor to greater electronic commerce? One answer for sure is that wireless and broadband technology will allow for anytime, anyplace communication and commerce. It's just that we don't quite yet know what the gadget will look like or how we will use it.

The Payers and Players Are Changing

The following are moving inexorably toward a new world of e-commerce:

- Subscriptions and Micropayments: The Internet will increasingly be fee-based.
- Changes in Search Engines: Information searching is the most important predictor of online buying and therefore profound changes will occur in the ways that search engines are structured.

Positive Globalization

"Globalization" is an undeniable trend against which people around the world are protesting because their lives, their cultures, and their futures have been and will continue to be affected. However, perhaps it is not "globalization" that is causing such anger and terror, but the unsettling fact that the Internet and technology are playing unprecedented roles in the advancement, decline, and reorganization of all economies and societies.

Worldwide manufacturing and sourcing strategies have made the production of goods cheaper, faster, and better. To compete internationally, producers around the globe must be able to measure levels of competitiveness and correct weaknesses. Doing so requires market information, an ability to understand and forecast demand, and creativity in product adaptation and market niching. These factors used to be a triple whammy against developing countries due to limited funds for research and development, scarcity of trade information, and unsophisticated marketing skills pervasive throughout these countries.

Information Technologies

Countries without efficient telecommunication infrastructure were seen as doomed and excluded from the benefits of electronic commerce to provide faster service and shipment, more precise order transmittal, on-line interaction in the production process, and global reach to prospective buyers.

Yet, not having up-to-date communication is no longer a permanent handicap. It used to be that governments regulated and controlled communication (and postal) services because only they could afford the expense. Today, however, the investment required to establish a basic national telecommunications system has decreased precipitously, allowing private firms to bring telecommunications to a country within just a few years. The question is therefore not if, but when, developing countries will participate in and benefit from global telecommunications.

Greater Cooperation with Developing Countries

The question remains: Will giant Internet firms such as Amazon and eBay destroy or help local competition in smaller and developing countries? Probably neither. One the most exciting trends and changes sure to occur is that prosperous countries such as the United States will no longer rely on trade and e-commerce between developed countries led by Fortune 500 corporations.

Indeed, e-commerce must increase in transition economies and developing countries if we are to benefit from a growing world economy. Policymakers and businesses of all sizes will soon realize that developing countries as diverse as Brazil, Chile, China, India, Kenya, the Philippines, Russia, and South Africa are strategically important, not just from a traditional sociopolitical perspective, They are also strategically important from the perspective of fostering a global integrated economic framework. It is in our collective best interest to respond to global trends that will foster growth in these and lesser developed countries. Why?

The answer is a simple fact: Firms in developing countries trading with firms in developed countries provide for expanded opportunities for investment and global electronic commerce. Thus they contribute to positive globalization through adoption of information technologies, and the forging of win-win-win partnerships and, often, triumvirates between businesses, government, and kindred organizations.

Win-Win-Win Partnerships and Networks

As developing countries foray more deeply into the global electronic economy, intense teamwork between business and government and among business people themselves has become imperative. Firms and governments have to bury their mistrust and foster constructive dialogue on strategies and effective collaboration.

And at the firm-to-firm level, businesses must begin to share costs and lessons learned. An emerging trend in the industrialized world is for firms to share costs of infrastructure, buildings, employees, storage, transport, repair, telecommunication systems, and, in some instances, marketing costs through dual or cross-promotion of complementary products.

Developing countries have to find their own models for such joint-ventures, value-added partnerships, strategic coalitions and alliances, and cooperative agreements. This is the wave of the future where risks are shared, vertical and horizontal networks are developed, and partnerships are king.

Enormous Opportunity for Exports . . . and Increased Competition

Despite many who believe e-commerce will be dominated by the US market, by the very nature of the Internet, e-commerce will contribute to the increase in global trade. In fact, non-US Internet surfers account for 86 percent of all Internet traffic worldwide, and more than 20 percent of the traffic on US-based sites come from outside the United States.

Companies around the globe will experience increased international competition because telecommunication, hardware, software, and Web design costs are no longer prohibitive. They will increasingly distribute to all countries dotting the globe. As a result, the Internet will reduce geographical barriers to entry, vastly increase the number of businesses around the globe, and increase the number of jobs in developing countries. Such change will result in a more equal and global economy, perhaps to the detriment of developed economies such as in the United States and Europe.

Rising and Falling Income Levels

If we think about this for a moment, it makes sense. The more people around the globe who have access to the Internet and technology, the greater the chances for economic growth.

Let us consider the fictional country Denica as an example of how the Internet and technology can contribute to "good globalization." Denica's economic growth was limited in the 20th century due to ethnic repression, attempted extermination of voiceless minority groups, and constant power struggles among these groups. Their government was corrupt and its ministries inert. Even though government had a monopoly control of its gas, oil, telephone, and other multimillion dollar industries, electricity supply was sporadic and expensive, water had to be boiled before people could drink it, and it would cost a day's wage to make a phone call to someone 100 kilometers away. Denica's people were mired in poverty, but some received paltry wages provided by multinational corporations because there were no alternatives for jobs. They either worked for five dollars a day in a factory or went without a job. Of course, education was important to the country, but students often used twenty-year-old books and were not learning about new inventions, modern history, computers, or business concepts.

Then something happened. The ethnic groups formed coalitions and started to work together to build honest government institutions. Monopolies were privatized, and basic services such as heat, electricity, water, and telephone and Internet access were greatly improved, not to mention much less expensive. Education improved immensely, and slowly people started to create their own businesses, manufacturing plants, and services. Over time, it just did not make economic sense for multinationals to remain in Denica because the people's wages were simply too high.

Now, imagine if this happened around the globe. Imagine what will happen when Argentina, Bangladesh, China, Costa Rica, Cuba, India, Jordan, Kenya, Mexico, Oman, Pakistan, Romania, Russia, Slovenia, South Africa, Tanzania, Turkey, Uganda, and Venezuela create better governments, infrastructure, and jobs for its people. Where would Gap, Nike, H&M Moritz, and thousands of other employers of cheap labor in developing countries go? Certainly to other countries. But as more and more countries democratize, liberalize, and increase the income levels of its citizens, the negative affects of US-dominated globalization will diminish because people in developing countries will create better jobs, and build their own clothing, computer, and car manufacturing businesses, if it is to their comparative advantage to do so.

In fact, it is happening already. I have been to each of these countries and have seen with my own eyes the positive results of liberalization, more accountable government, and a peaceful society. Certainly it will take generations in some countries, but the point is that it is happening and the Internet can only help.

But, readers in the United States and Europe may be thinking, "If individuals in Latin America, Africa, the Middle East, Far East, and Asia start creating their own clothing, computer, and car manufacturing businesses, where do we export our things and where do we find cheap labor? What happens to my standard of living?"

Although it is not the purpose of the book to focus on these larger issues, the question is important enough to answer. Perhaps the answer is, as the Internet helps to globalize the economy in a good way, perhaps all of our incomes will rise and fall. They will surely rise in developing countries that have good democracies and good job opportunities for its people. And they will surely drop for people in developed countries who relied on developing countries for access to cheap goods.

As a result, after generations of inequity, the gap between the developed and developing countries will surely decrease, and, at the same time, the rising tide will raise all our ships. The larger questions remain as to when and where it will happen first but one thing is for certain: the Internet will vastly change the global economy in the 21st century.

But how? What kinds of policies, programs, and services need to be developed to truly make electronic commerce a positive force for all of us? Are you a solider, general, friend or foe of the 21st-century technology revolution? Will you join the protest against change or be a thought leader to create a better world through the use of the Internet and technology?

Emergence of Technology Pioneers

The rate of technological advances is not an even, expanding one. It is an exponential growth that is exploding. In recognition of the contributions that technology has made to humankind, the World Economic Forum and Deloitte Touche Tohmatsu have selected the world's most innovative "Technology Pioneers" each year since 2000 (see Exhibit 6.2). The pioneers are chief executives who developed and applied innovative

EXHIBIT 6.2 Representative World Economic Forum 2002 Tech Pioneers

Anoto AB, Sweden combined the first ballpoint pen incorporating Bluetooth wireless technology with the first specialized, communications-friendly digital paper.

AstroPower, USA makes and sells photovoltaic solar cells, modules, panels and SunChoice systems used for converting sunlight into electricity.

BlueArc Corporation, USA delivers network storage systems designed to change the way firms implement their IT infrastructures, allowing them to exploit their optical networks fully while dramatically lowering the total cost of ownership.

ChangingWorlds, Ireland has advanced personalization technologies with a focus on digital TV and mobile/wireless markets. The ClixSmart personalization engine enables this intelligent information service to learn about the needs and preferences of users and to personalize the delivery and presentation of information content to individuals automatically.

CommercialWare, Inc., USA is a provider of software solutions for multi-channel retailer that allows retailers to interact, transact with and service their customers across multiple channels, ensuring high levels of customer satisfaction and loyalty.

Corvis Corporation, USA enables telecommunications service providers to construct manageable all-optical networks that will accommodate the growth of Internet, video, voice and other data traffic.

CSR (Cambridge Silicon Radio), United Kingdom designs and manufactures single-chip radio devices, focusing on solutions for the 2.4 GHz Bluetooth personal area networking standard.

Cytokinetics, USA focused on the complementary missions of drug discovery and the commercialization of novel cellular bioinformatics technologies.

Danger Research, USA has an end-to-end wireless Internet solution focused on affordability and great user experience. The Danger solution tightly integrates service, platform and hardware and will be introduced to the mass market through partnerships with established consumer brands.

Digital Envoy, USA has a geo-targeting program that allows customers to target and restrict Web content on a geographic basis, worldwide, down to a city-level.

E Ink Corporation, USA is the developer of electronic ink for use in point-of-sale signs in retail stores, next generation displays in mobile telecommunications devices and PDAs, and thin, portable electronic books and newspapers.

EXHIBIT 6.2 (Continued)

Gopher Publishers, The Netherlands has a Publishing-and-Printing-on-Demand concept by means of 100 percent Web-based publishing.

Medis Technologies, USA developed proprietary technologies for cleaner and more efficient energy, including fuel cells for portable energy sources.

Microvision, Inc., USA develops light scanning technologies that, when integrated into handheld or headworn devices, project images onto the retina of the eye, allowing an individual to see large, full-motion images without the need for a screen.

Myriad Genetics, Inc., USA provides bioinformatic gene mapping, family history analysis and protein interaction identification to find inherited gene mutations that increase the risk for cancer, heart attacks, and other diseases.

netLibrary, Inc., USA is a provider of electronic books (eBooks) helping academic, public, corporate, and special libraries create a richer, more productive learning environment.

PayPal, USA is an instant and secure online payment service.

Red-M, United Kingdom develops hardware and software to allow mobile data, voice, and video communications inside buildings and public concourses for computers, personal digital assistants, wireless application protocol smart phones, and other emerging information appliances, all using wireless Bluetooth technology.

RiboTargets Ltd., United Kingdom is a pharmaceutical company that specializes in anti-infective research and development. Its therapeutic interests include anti-bacterial and antiviral agents, including HIV and Hepatitis C.

Rolltronics, USA developed a manufacturing technique called "roll-to-roll" or "web" processing. Roll-to-roll processing is used to produce a new class of thin-film electronics that are created directly on flexible substrates. These can include semiconductors, circuit boards and flat panel displays.

Source: McCue's research and discussion with the World Economic Forum.

and transformational technologies in fields such as proteomics, peer-to-peer, renewable energy, and Internet infrastructure to illustrate how technologies can be used to finally bridge the digital divide, create economic growth, and enhance global communication. Technology Pioneers are selected based on innovation, growth and sustainability, proof of concept, leadership, and potential impact.

General Trends

In the 1980s, microcomputers made it economically feasible for businesses to process their own data; in the 1990s, the Internet allowed data to be connected. Also in the 1990s, wireless telephones arrived, greatly increasing the availability of telephones in developing countries. Liberalization of market policies allowed a more rapid growth of telephony infrastructure, and more competitive pricing of services.

In the next decade, microprocessors will be embedded in many more devices connected via wireless technology. We will expect to see an increased use of ICT in small appliances, personal services, and within the human body. Theft will become virtually impossible due to virtually invisible radio-frequency identification (RFID) tags being placed on humans, animals, vehicles, and anything else of value. ICT will become increasingly embedded in goods and services, will improve the production processes, underlie a revolution in management techniques that increase enterprise efficiency and effectiveness, and will modify the linkages between enterprises and others, including clients, suppliers, collaborators, competitors, and government. They can be applied to virtually every function of the firm, including marketing, finance, human resource management, and production management.

Similar to having the ability to lead a horse to water, but a great inability in having it drink, a business can be wired with the greatest ICT but too often have a great inability to force the use of information to improve efficiency and effectiveness. Businesses everywhere face a huge task in training people to use ICT, reengineer organizational structures, and reengineering processes to use ICT effectively.

7

Enhance Your EQ* . . . Education for the 21st Century

Millions of managers are still adjusting to the new knowledge requirements for conducting business in the 21st century. Just what do you need to know to survive and thrive in the new e-conomy? What will you need to know to enhance your EQ?

Those who have a high EQ will have high employability in the future. The demand for people with e-commerce savvy will continue to grow, as will the compensation packages.

The elements that go into achieving a high EQ are addressed in this book. You've already taken the first step onto—or are well on your way on—the learning "curve." That curve, as you may have already surmised, will not ever go downward; nor will it ever end, because of the continuous changes and improvements. But as more and more businesses, governments, and associations adapt their ways to profit from the Internet and its potential, you will find a place for you and your skills.

What You Need to Know

With the advent of e-commerce and the Internet, a new generation of managers, planners, analysts, and programmers must be educated and trained on the realities and potential for all forms of e-commerce among industrial, commercial, governmental, institutional, and consumer

---

*EQ (E-Commerce Quotient): parallel to IQ.

participants. In the early 21st-century global economy, managers must know how to:

- Appraise electronic trade and commerce opportunities in precise terms of costs and benefits.
- Construct a variety of complete electronic commerce systems for selling products and services.
- Construct systems for managing vendor relations.
- Appraise tools such as hypertext transfer protocol (HTTP) servers, secure transaction software and firewalls, low and high-end database systems, heterogeneous networks, network news transfer protocol (NNTP) servers, client software, financial institution networking tools, and intelligent agents.
- Draft contracts needed to support electronic trade and commerce on the Internet.
- Provide the financial accounting infrastructure to support electronic trade and commerce.

The following are key skills needed for 21st-century business:

Site design for marketing
Site design for systems integration
Automated e-procurement systems
Communications and networking
Marketing
Marketing research
Web-based information architectures
Finance and financial accounting
Electronic payment systems
Computer security
E-commerce systems design
Supply chain management
E-commerce law and regulation
Pricing
Information systems development
Order fulfillment
Multimedia
Databases
Electronic negotiation
Intelligent agents
Online customer service and help facilities

Mobile e-commerce
Language technologies in e-commerce
Cultural differences

E-Commerce Management

Managers will need to be able to conduct strategic analyses of what has changed and will be changing at the industry level and then how e-marketing and e-service have changed and will be changing in the context of B2B commerce and supply chain management.

E-Commerce Technology: Do You Know How All This Works?

Managers must be knowledgeable of the technologies relevant to electronic commerce including communications and networking, the Internet and mobile e-commerce, the architecture of Web systems, data interchange, access and cryptographic security, electronic payments, databases, multimedia, mass personalization, search engines, data mining and intelligent agents. Also, managers must be familiar with Java programming, with particular emphasis on e-commerce applications to understand object-oriented programming, and write Java programs, Swing graphical user Interfaces (GUIs), and applets.

Communications and Networking

How is information transferred in a fraction of a second from Sydney to San Francisco? To "talk the talk," managers should be familiar on a basic level with the principles underlying the interconnection of large numbers of computers including intranets and internets; transmission technologies, such as ethernet, optical fiber, gigabit networks, cellular transmission, and infrared; and network technologies such as servers, clients, and access control. So, if you don't understand the hardware and interface components of a computerized communications network, and understand the software required to support a network, you'll get gouged by high-priced technologists who will likely sell you systems that are too large and/or not responsive to your needs.

The Internet

The Internet is the largest and most highly distributed information system ever created. Do you understand the basic technology of the Internet and its important applications, including the World Wide Web?

You should have a basic familiarity with internetworking, Internet Protocol (IP) internetworking, the global IP Internet, client-server computing, Internet client-server applications, Web technology, techniques for building secure, scalable, and highly available Internet servers, and XML technology. So that you can "talk technical" and run your business according to your technical needs, you should be conversant in how a Linux Web Server is built and be able to demonstrate familiarity with TCP/IP, UDP, DNS, SMTP, HTTP, HTML, XML.

E-Marketing Fundamentals

What is an e-commerce/e-marketing strategy? Do you understand the difference between traditional and e-commerce-based buyer behavior? How should you set your price online and offline? Is there any difference in your distribution, advertising, or promotion strategies?

Marketing Research

Implementation of e-business systems requires market research on a large scale, but it's been made possible—and manageable—by the Internet. The development, implementation, and monitoring compliance required by a successful business today calls for processing large amounts of information about the company environment: customers, present competitors and potential entrants, suppliers, legal developments, various constituencies. And much, much more. All of these are now available on the Internet and will help you more easily implement an electronic research program design.

Web-Based Information Architectures

Are you familiar with the design, creation, instrumentation, and usage of sites and related indexing and searching software? To be successful in e-commerce, you should know how to use search engines, how to design e-commerce sites that maximize customer attraction via search engines, how to analyze competition, the structure of information architectures, and how to design both topological and key-term page access paths.

You should also have a passing familiarity with how search engines are created, including inverted-indexing, partial matching, query-expansion, and spidering technology; automated text categorization (i.e., indexing Web pages into Yahoo!-like taxonomies or auction-site catalogs), information extraction from Web-pages, and larger-scale text and data mining methods.

Finance and Financial Accounting

Don't want to be the next Ken Lay, the CEO of Enron whose financial wizards created complex accounting systems that bankrupted the largest energy company in the world? Then you should be able to read basic domestic financial statements. A basic understanding of the four primary financial statements involves understanding the balance sheet, the income statement, the statement of cash flows, and the statement of retained earnings. You should also understand specific line items in the income statement and balance sheet including revenue recognition, current assets (including accounts receivable and inventories), non-current assets, current liabilities, non-current liabilities (including bonds and leases), inter-corporate investments and business combinations, and income taxes.

On a basic level, you should understand the time value of money and compounding, capital budgeting, portfolio theory and diversification, risk and return, capital structure and dividend policy, and the term structure of interest rates in order to be able to compute the return on investment of an e-commerce system.

Electronic Payment Systems

As an e-commerce manager, you should know the difference between the properties of money and electronic payment systems, fiduciary *v.* scriptural money, token *v.* notational money, cash and "real money," and related payment risks. In terms of banking systems and foreign exchange, you should know what banks do, what the role of central banks is, and how money is transferred. You should also be aware of the forms of electronic money; automated clearing and settlement systems; e-payment security (cryptographic methods, hash functions, etc); digital certificates, including certificate chains and public-key infrastructure; and credit card security and related SSL and SET protocols. Also, managers should be aware of the characteristics of micro-payment systems, electronic cash, and electronic invoicing.

Computer Security

The basis of e-commerce is an infrastructure for providing reliable transactions in which payments and products are directed properly without risk of interception or tampering. Do you know how you can assure your customers they will receive a genuine, secure, and confidential transmission of information across networks? Become familiar with basic principles of digital cryptography and public-key cryptosystems, cryptographic standards (e.g., Data Encryption Standard, or DES), government security policy, digital signatures, digital escrow, certification, and secure communications and secure hardware. You should also have a familiarity with how password attacks occur and how to detect and remove a virus.

E-Commerce Systems Design

Are you familiar with the life-cycle issues involved in specifying, designing and implementing software architecture for e-commerce? If yes, you are aware of both technical concepts (e.g., object-oriented design, multi-tier architectures) and management concepts (e.g., software project estimation, specification and design, planning, management).

Supply Chain Management

Do you know how to use information and communication technology for online supply chain management? It's more than knowing who is in the chain. It involves focusing on management of raw materials and finished inventory to maximize return on investment; the interrelationship of obtaining materials, working on and storing materials and products internally; delivering products to their final destination in the face of uncertainty; changing prices, and varying demands. Managers of e-commerce-oriented businesses should also understand how to prepare online inventory and reorder policies, fulfill and ship orders placed online, and create online systems to deal with peak and slack demands.

E-Commerce Law and Regulation

How much do you know—need to know—about the legal and policy environment of e-commerce? Because it is constantly evolving and changing, you should know the basic legal concepts and functioning of the courts as well as how to:

- Protect online intellectual property and advertising techniques.
- Protect yourself and your customers from online fraud.
- Enforce electronic agreements.
- Understand securities regulation, taxation, antitrust, criminal law, and international law.

Pricing

As you know, price is the only marketing mix variable that directly generates revenue; all others involve costs. Still, pricing for Internet sales is one of the least understood and most controversial aspects of marketing. Are you familiar with popular online pricing practices and do you understand their pitfalls?

Information Systems Development

Today computers are having major impacts on how managers make decisions and how companies compete successfully in the marketplace. Do you have the ability to use information systems effectively and exploit information technology for productive purposes? Managers should understand how information systems are developed and deployed, evaluate the feasibility of proposed information systems projects, and determine the information required to make more effective decisions.

Order Fulfillment

Many e-commerce systems are distributed order-entry systems directed at the individual retail purchaser, while others are for large-scale business-to-business transactions. In both cases, order fulfillment is critical because of how easy it is for electronic customers to change loyalties. Both the purchaser and supplier need the ability to track orders even after they have left the supplier's control. Are you able to create a chain of procedures and information systems that lead to efficient, trackable order fulfillment that is crucial to the success of e-commerce? If yes, you will be able to integrate an e-commerce system with other systems in the supply and fulfillment chain and develop a comprehensive e-business design capable of delivering the orders it receives.

Multimedia

Until recent years, most computing tasks dealt with numerical, text, and symbolic data, and the field of computer science emphasized these data types. Digital representations of audio, video, and images are now becoming quite common. With the advent of cheaper and larger online storage capacities, fast network transmission speeds and advances in digital compression, comprehensive sources of multiple media (text, image, video and audio) can be easily stored and made available. Collecting and intelligently integrating these multiple media opens up opportunities for novel business applications. Consequently, an understanding of multimedia is essential for many e-commerce businesses. How can you easily capture, process, compress, search, index, store, and retrieve various kinds of continuous media?

Databases

Larger information systems usually employ multiple computers. Are you familiar with the types of these systems and how to satisfy requirements for availability, reliability, interoperability, and scale? In order to talk technical with the experts who know this stuff, you should have a passing familiarity with schema design, query processing, file systems, multimedia databases, and the interconnection of databases to other information systems.

Electronic Negotiation

Electronic negotiation takes place very rapidly in a world that is rich in information that may be inconsistent, incorrect, or misleading. You should be aware of the finer points of negotiating electronically, both by human interaction and through automated agents known as bots. Also, there are English, Dutch, Vickrey, single sealed-bid, and runoff auctions of which you should be aware.

Intelligent Agents

A software agent is a software module that runs more or less autonomously and that provides a specific service for human users or for other software. Agents have important applications in e-commerce. For example, a software agent may run continuously searching the Web for news stories on a certain topic or comparing prices posted online for a certain brand of automobile. A collection of relatively simple agents, perhaps running on many different machines, can often handle that which was formerly performed by large, monolithic software systems that were difficult to build and very hard to understand and modify. But while agent-based systems can be very powerful and intuitive, there can be problems. For example, if one agent becomes overloaded or ceases to operate, a system could fail unless provision is made for backup and recovery. Do you know what to do when this happens?

Customer Service and Help Facilities

Electronic commerce requires electronic assistance. In a traditional retail setting, salespeople and information representatives are available to help the customer and guide him or her toward a purchase. In the electronic world, it is all too easy for a frustrated consumer to switch to a different site. How will you help customers electronically to ensure that they have all questions promptly answered, obtain help even without specifically requesting it, interact with a system that understands the consumer's habits and preferred modes of navigation, and allow them to complain to the appropriate human source if they are dissatisfied?

Do you and your sales staff need to learn how to respond in a timely and effective manner to inquiries and problems of the Web shop and marketplace customers? Training usually involves explaining how to respond with an e-mail or telephone call to address customer concerns. In more advanced and thoroughly automated e-commerce systems, customer service can be achieved through an automated e-mail assistance program in which the software responds directly to your customers, automatically checking and reporting back the status of your customers' order within your production cycle. Refer to DHL's order tracking system at http://www.dhl.com to gain an idea of an efficient, easy, and customer-friendly system.

Mobile E-Commerce

According to UseageWatch.org, by mid-2004 the number of mobile phone subscriptions was nearly 1.5 billion (out of a total worldwide population of over 6 billion), or double the number in 2000. Developing countries account for this sharp growth—56% of all mobile phone subscribers and 79% of overall growth since 2000:

- China had 310M mobile phone subscribers by mid-2004.
- Russia had 60M subscribers, with an 80% growth in one year.
- India had 44.5M subscribes, with a 25% increase by 2005.

In the meantime, the number of fixed lines has increased from 1 billion in 2000 to 1.185 billion in 2005.

"M-commerce" covers the explosion of applications and services that will become accessible from Internet-enabled mobile devices. It involves new technologies, services, and business models, and is different from "traditional" e-commerce. Mobile phones or personal digital assistants

(PDAs) impose very different constraints than desktop computers, but they also open the door to a slew of new applications and services for consumers and enterprises. They will likely start generating tens of billions of US dollars a year in revenue within the next few years. Are you familiar with the technologies, applications, services, and new business models associated with m-commerce?

Language Technologies in E-Commerce

Language processing over the Internet for global electronic commerce is a huge issue, including how to represent alphabets and character sets on Web pages, transmit content over the Internet in multiple languages, machine translation, text summarization and voice recognition. On a cultural level, managers should also design multilingual sites that do not offend, create trust, and can select appropriate dialogue patterns. Are you familiar with the degrees of politeness in different cultures (e.g., Japanese), gender differences, formal vs. informal register (German Du vs. Sie), and the avoidance of, or the need for, imperatives?

How to Approach Cultural Aspects

Do you and your staff understand your role in relation to the new e-commerce system? Depending on how you choose to program your systems, the role of the sales staff may be minimized with existing customers. Some e-commerce options will allow transactions to pass automatically to the production system, thus redefining the role of the sales agent in reporting back to the customer on production capacity and in placing the final resulting order. Finance staff could also save time with e-commerce systems that automatically enter order information into a firm's financial software system. Commerce staff could save time with e-commerce systems that automatically update production schedules and commerce needs.

How to Use Technology

Staff in each department will have to be trained on understanding data management, analysis, and sharing relevant to their jobs. For example, finance staff will need to understand how to read and integrate incoming data forms into existing budget documents. Sales agents will have to understand how incoming order forms affect available inventory, and how to access this information on the system for reference while selling. Are you prepared to arrange for training of the production staff who will need to know exactly which processes are automatically engaged and which require manual input?

How to Promote Your Products Electronically

Do you and your staff know how to promote your products on your company site as well as on electronic marketplaces? Marketing on the Web can be done either in tandem with a programmer, or manually by staff trained in marketing.

How to Bill Customers and Get Paid

Do you and your finance staff know the protocols for managing online payments, often via financials software? This software will have interfaces with your other internal systems, such as sales and production. It will also become connected to your external customers' payment systems.

How to Conduct Marketplace Research

You and your staff should continuously search the Web for trends regarding company home pages, new electronic marketplaces, and developments in the marketplace by reading publications and industry reports available on analyst sites.

How to Participate in Buy-Side and Supply-Side Online Auctions

Do you know how to monitor electronic transactions and marketplace traffic to ensure there are no failures within the system?

The underlying emphasis is that you will learn and learn some more and learn more yet, about communications between and among similar and differing cultures, technology developments, new processes, and coping and growing with change. Knowing about e-commerce is not for the faint-hearted, but it is for all those people who want to—and must— keep abreast with what's happening in the world today and what could be happening in the future. It's quite an adventure!

8

Actions for Thought Leaders

Fostering a Hospitable Climate

In order for more businesses to adapt electronic commerce and information and communication technology into their everyday business operations, business managers, government agencies, universities, technical training programs, and consulting programs must work together to help businesses participate in the electronic economy.

Certainly "the market" will evolve by learning from the e-commerce survivors and thrivers. Software programs will develop more affordable, common sensical technology that can be easily integrated. "Government" will address financial, legal, and other policy issues related to electronic commerce, including encryption, security of payments, taxation, certification and authentication, confidentiality, intellectual property protection, fraud and consumer protection, and access to telecommunications and connectivity. And universities will begin to emulate the first movers who have developed modern business curricula in response to students' need to understand 21st century business.

But e-commerce will more quickly evolve, improve, and contribute to an improved economy if these groups work together to address *how* greater use of the Internet and ICT can be fostered among smaller businesses everywhere in particular. It is imperative that these groups work together to address how the Internet can benefit them, and to train them on how to use the Internet as a sales, marketing, communication, and supply management medium.

Business managers, technologists, government policy makers, university professors, trainers, and consultants must join hands to respond to the needs and constraints of smaller enterprises; otherwise e-commerce will continue to be a medium that confounds, confuses, and does not reach its potential to irrevocably alter traditional business practices.

Who Should Care?

Thought leaders on the national, regional, state, and local levels should form groups to meet on a regular basis to identify specific problems, opportunities and strategies to foster communication among the private and public sector, understand who is doing what, and determine key trends and need for concerted action. This coalition of representatives from all sectors involved in e-commerce should address the challenges, trends, and constraints inherent to this new medium. By working together rather than separately, the members of the group will not only be more efficient in solving problems, they will also reap, individually and collectively, the benefits from their efforts sooner than if they were to attempt to work on their own.

Among those who *should* care about e-commerce are:

Banks
Business media writers
Chambers of commerce
Customs officials
Development agencies
Enterprises, large and small
Freight forwarders
Government agencies
Information, communications and telecommunications industry
Internet service providers
Legal experts
National industry associations
Software designers and vendors
Universities and training institutes
Vendors of computer equipment
Web site designers

The most critical issues we still face are how to:

- Improve and develop ICT infrastructure.
- Develop model policy and enabling legislation.
- Address regulatory and security issues.

- Create public and private sector partnerships and network building.

It is equally important, however, to foster a greater awareness and real knowledge among businesses regarding e-commerce, conduct practical research on issues that matter to businesses, and develop practical and impactful consulting services and training programs. These efforts will expand economic opportunities, create jobs, and increase export opportunities using electronic commerce.

It is clear that no one person can possibly claim to be an expert in all of these issues. While someone may be an "expert" on the transactional aspect of e-commerce, others may be experts in e-marketing, Web design, ensuring secure transactions, etc. Therefore, bringing together a diverse group of experts on the various aspects of electronic commerce will result in:

- Awareness building of the group (to get to know "who is doing what").
- Greater understanding of the informational, technical and legal constraints facing businesses (and to assess the needs of small- and medium-sized exporters).
- Greater understanding of where their areas and their countries are headed with respect to their national e-commerce strategy.

Finally, we hope that this group will review the list in this chapter of nearly 100 programs and services and decide what each organization will do as part of an overall strategy. Because most interests will have been represented, a diverse group will be part of an overall strategy.

Who Should Sit at the Table?

Overall, the "thought leaders" should be respected professionals within the business, exporting, and e-commerce community. They should be good communicators with a willingness to collaborate and educate others in their respective professions. These professions include:

- Banking Professionals. These are people with knowledge of secure online payment options and standardized payment procedures for international transactions.
- Business Writers from the Mass and Trade Media. E-commerce and technology matters in the press are often confusing because often writers do not understand the constantly changing phe-

nomena called e-commerce as well as the related information and communication technology. The purposes for having the media involved is to so that they know more about and understand better the overall programs and services available for businesses, to provide their perspectives, and to contribute and support the development of an overall strategy.

- Chambers of Commerce. As organizations composed of businesses varying in size and industry, chambers of commerce have perspectives and connections that are invaluable.

- Designers and Vendors of Software. The development and distribution of appropriate e-commerce and ICT software is critically important to the improvement in the use of appropriate and relevant technology for e-commerce transactions.

- Development Organizations. Representatives would provide input and feedback on the overall strategy and on the financial and human resources needed for particular action items. They should be able to help the group realistically estimate its financial needs based on human and physical assets required.

- Enterprises, Large and Small. Most businesses are unclear how they can benefit from the Internet and information and communication technologies to improve business organization, communication, marketing and sales. Therefore, representatives of businesses (not large firms employing more than 100 people) should be able to share questions, experiences, and concerns from business, organizational, and government perspectives.

- Freight Forwarding and/or Customs Professionals. The freight forwarding and/or customs professionals should have the ability to explain trends, opportunities, and challenges in processing and shipping goods using electronic mediums.

- Government Agencies. High-level representatives of all pertinent government agencies should be able to provide overall feedback and advice as it relates to often unknown and/or misunderstood goals of the government. These individuals should also be willing to deliver information and convey questions back to decision-makers within the government.

- Internet Service Providers. The ISP representative should be able to communicate problems and solutions in how to increase the connectivity rate and improve e-commerce transactions.

- Legal Experts. Representatives from the legal sector should be able to convey the international, national, and/or local legal frameworks for e-commerce, dispute settlement, legality of electronic contracts, electronic signatures, and protecting business interests. They should also have general knowledge of taxation issues.

- National Exporters Associations. A representative from the National Exporters Association should be able to provide an overall perspective of the needs of exporters. This individual should also be aware of the vast array of exporting and e-commerce programs and services offered throughout the country and, in particular, offered by its association.

- National Industry/Sector Associations. As many representatives of sector associations as possible should be included. Sector-specific associations should be selected based on the potential for certain industries to grow using e-commerce (e.g., food processing, under-capacity manufacturers, tourism industry, call center support, indigenous products, or emerging services, etc.) Representatives of these industries should be familiar with e-commerce trends, opportunities, and limitations in these sectors.

- Software Designers and Vendors. As the "translator" of user needs into workable software on individual and mass scales, the designers/programmers know the pitfalls, performance and potential of what users would like to have. The insights of software vendors are valuable because they are in the "middle" between designers and dreamers.

- Vendors of Hardware. Clearly, the ability for businesses to improve the availability and quality of their computing equipment is critical to the development of e-commerce in any country, including the United States. The ratio of personal computers per 1000 people in a country ranges from 2.5 in Uganda; 9.1 in Indonesia; 33.7; Colombia; 44.2 in Mexico; 360 in Canada; 376 in the United States; and 437 in Singapore. The representative should be able to offer innovative ideas and know of solutions in other countries as to how to increase the number of computers in use.

- Universities, National Training Institutes, Technical Colleges. Representatives from training institutes, technical colleges, and universities should be able to provide an overview of the current research being undertaken on electronic commerce for businesses, express the questions and concerns of their students, and/or have experience in offering training programs or seminars on the topic of electronic commerce.

- Web Site Designers. Experienced site designers should be able to provide practical experiences on opportunities and technical difficulties inherent in designing Web sites.

E-Commerce Deliberations: A Workable Strategy

Although such a group can come together for many reasons, at its core the group should have the following goals as a minimum:

- Specific Objectives or Actions. The group should create a strategy for growth in e-commerce through partnerships, benchmarks, and a diversified funding base for developing programs and services that respond to needs.
- A Roadmap. The report of the group's deliberations and recommendations should serve as a framework and guide to future development in the area of e-commerce. The report represents a working consensus on goals, strategies, programs, roles and responsibilities.
- Enhanced Communication. The group should set up mechanisms to ensure that consistent and accurate information on development, growth, and accomplishments in the area of e-commerce enterprises will be deliverable to the community.
- Coordinated Activities with E-Commerce Service Providers. Without a seamless delivery system of related organizations, needs will not be met.

Essential Elements of the Strategy

At issue is the essence of defining the role of the public and private sectors that are dedicated to improving the performance of business in the global economy. This is characterized by instantaneous communication, shared technology, and abundant (but not always reliable) sources of information. In order to answer questions, the group must identify strategies and operational plans, identify opportunities, and shape the future of the community's e-commerce development through focused, practical, and concerted action.

The core of the e-commerce strategy should be an array of product, publication and service offerings that can be provided to enterprises when they need it and where they are, and do it in a format that is user-friendly, comprehensive, cost effective, and is responsive to their clearly identified needs and constraints.

Articulating the Vision

As the discussions evolve, they should focus on at least the following primary areas:

- Public/private partnerships and network building.
- Targeted sectors for e-commerce growth and development.
- Goals to improve infrastructure.
- Development of conducive legislation, sound regulations, and trust-building security measures.
- Human resource development.
- Financing and grant programs.

Public/Private Partnerships and Network Building

Commitment, cooperation, coordination, and communication among the members of this pivotal group are imperative to stimulate e-commerce. Integrated actions undertaken by these groups are vital to ensuring the success of the initiative.

Targeted Sectors for E-Commerce Growth and Development

As previously mentioned, the Internet and e-commerce can benefit literally thousands of industries. Therefore, it is important to identify sector-specific industries in which they would like to focus for strategic export-led growth.

Targeting sectors can be perceived as "picking winners," or focusing on sectors that do not really need help because they are already prospering in e-commerce. On the other hand, nurturing poorly performing sectors may be perceived as wasting precious time and financial resources. As a result, many organizations find it difficult to segment sectors that can be developed because:

- They don't know which sectors have e-commerce growth potential.
- Elected officials demand provision of services to all constituencies, especially because e-commerce is so new to all sectors.

- Economic development organizations and training institutes are incapable of identifying and communicating with businesses within a particular sector due to poor data mining, mailing list maintenance and update, and outreach and awareness-building techniques.

Unable to respond to these issues, organizations simply find it easier to offer all e-commerce service to all sectors. This "reactive" rather than "proactive" approach to the provision of counseling, training, research, publications, and advocacy to all businesses within a particular area or country is simply inefficient and ineffective.

You can achieve effective targeting, segmenting, and prioritizing of your client base through:

- Sound market research and buyer needs analysis, to identify existing and emerging opportunities for using ICT.
- An e-commerce strategy that targets sectors for e-commerce and export-led economic growth.
- "Picking winners" instead of "nurturing losers" (i.e., focusing on sector-specific niches rather than providing all e-commerce services to all businesses).
- Selecting five to ten sectors that will be targets.
- Providing assistance only to those businesses that have met stringent criteria for assistance in e-commerce (e.g., number of employees, profit/loss ratio, number of years successfully exporting, within targeted sectors, etc.).

Goals to Improve Infrastructure

It is widely viewed that without a liberalized (i.e., deregulated) telecommunications sector, the necessary infrastructure for e-commerce will not be developed. Privatizing and liberalizing the telecommunications market allows the government to participate fully in the telecommunication and digital revolution occurring before our eyes (and ears) in partnership with proven leaders in the often changing, volatile telecommunication and information technology industry. Privatizing also provides for economies of scale, reduced rates for Internet access, increase in the number of ISPs, and improved customer service through application of state-of-the-art 21st-century technologies.

It is axiomatic that the government would also generate increased tax revenue regarding the expansion of Internet service throughout the country. Greater diversification of the national ICT market correlates to a vastly improved infrastructure within the country, allowing businesses to expand into foreign markets, such as B2B, B2C, and B2G e-commerce.

So ask what policies are being designed to encourage the development of high speed, high bandwidth infrastructure for commercial use at competitive prices. The increasing demand for efficient, low-cost telecommunication services is higher than ever in today's service-oriented, Internet-based economy. Maintaining barriers to market entry by not improving basic infrastructure makes little sense for a country interested in developing a national e-commerce strategy.

Development of telecommunications and purpose-built physical facilities to increase the competitiveness of the ICT industry, and the productivity of workers should be clearly discussed and detailed in the summary of the overall strategy.

Development of Conducive Legislation, Sound Regulations, and Trust-Building Security Measures

A successful e-commerce strategy requires the establishment of a supportive regulatory framework for ICT and e-commerce and the streamlining of procedures to ensure secure transactions. Development and implementation of a comprehensive e-commerce law is an important national and local priority and is essential for the long-term competitiveness of a country's industries. And the prerequisite for e-commerce is a safe, secure, and efficient e-banking mechanism that allows payments and financial transactions between banks, consumers, and merchants to be performed legally and safely via the Internet.

Legal issues include, but are not limited to:

- The overall national legal framework.
- How the strategy addresses international legal frameworks for e-commerce.
- How cross-border electronic disputes will be settled.
- The binding and legality of contracts made electronically, electronic signatures, and
- Protecting copyrights, domain names, etc., that are published on the Internet.

Human Resource Development

Long-term competitiveness depends on the ability of primary and secondary educational system, training institutes, and technical colleges to produce the quality and quantity of e-commerce and ICT professionals to meet requirements of the overall e-commerce strategy.

The group's e-commerce strategy document should include measures that will be undertaken for working with universities, training institutes, and technical colleges which focus on critical IT and e-commerce skills and knowledge development. Also, it is important to highlight any e-commerce research initiatives being undertaken to better understand the export-oriented e-commerce economy.

Financing and Grant Programs

Innovative mechanisms may be required to provide funding to the targeted industries (including the domestic information and communication technology sector) and to provide the necessary equipment in order for the businesses to conduct e-commerce.

Questions to Consider When Preparing the Group's E-Commerce Strategy

In light of the many constraints facing businesses of any size, how can a successful strategy be formulated for e-commerce and e-government? The Web is fast becoming the principal tool to provide business information, to communicate with enterprises, and to market organizational programs and services. How can the group's members respond to the online informational needs of industry, and help enterprises become bigger, better, faster, and smarter? What are the programs and services that can be designed in response to the needs of smaller businesses? In sum, how have clients, products, services, and delivery mechanisms changed because of the Internet?

When preparing the e-commerce strategy, members of the group should provide cogent answers to at least the following questions. While the first two are the most fundamental questions facing us who view e-commerce as a way to increase sales using the Internet, the latter must also be addressed:

- How can our organizations foster e-commerce among smaller enterprises?
- What are the programs and services our organizations should

develop? How can smaller enterprises be seen among 800 million Web sites?

- How can they use information technology to create efficiencies and economies of scale?
- What are the things that government should do that the private sector cannot? How can the private sector be involved?
- How can each member of partner organizations become more involved to provide counseling, training, research, and information?
- How can enterprises be encouraged to use the Internet as a sales, marketing, research, communication and supply management medium?
- What are the specific needs and constraints facing enterprises? The strategy must respond to needs, not demands. Enterprises say they need money, computers, and site designers, but don't they also need help crafting an e-commerce plan, industry-specific alliances, and incubators to share costs?
- What kinds of awareness-building campaigns can be undertaken to debunk myths? There are scores of myths, misperceptions, and myopic attitudes regarding the Internet that constantly arise.
- Multinational corporations need smaller enterprises and vice versa, but how can they work together?
- If lower-cost computers are needed, how can multinationals be convinced to sell computers at a lower price? How can win-win-win agreements be negotiated?
- How can training seminars and conferences respond to needs, not just deliver more hype about the importance of the Internet?
- What are the incentives that work for smaller enterprises? Do they include micro loans, grants for Web design, etc.? How can they be quantified?
- What is a model national portal site? Is a national portal for smaller business information helpful, harmful, or necessary? If the answers are yes, no, and yes, then what is to be the content of the site? How will members of the group come to agreement on this important issue?
- To match buyers with suppliers, how can importers and exporters use national or industry-specific product and company online registers?
- Will universities or other organizations develop key performance

indicators for an effective site? Time and again, smaller enterprises say they want case studies to evaluate effectiveness, identify effective techniques, and determine effective hit/leads/sales ratios.

- How can those who have been successful on the Web be matched with aspiring e-entrepreneurs?
- What is the university's role in the e-commerce development by smaller businesses?
- Who is researching why more consumers are not buying online?
- How do buyers want to receive online marketing messages?
- How can online customer service be improved?
- What are the constraints within government that hinder development of a national e-commerce strategy?
- What organization(s) will disseminate online trade leads and how can enterprises be helped to make sense of the data? To be sure, trade lead and export-import statistics are included on many country's sites, but how can you help the business identify trends and target markets using data provided online?
- What kinds of e-mail-based virtual discussion conferences will be offered? Using e-mail communication to encourage enterprises to talk to each other to share ideas, successes, and issues is extremely helpful. Will organizations in your community take the time to offer these extremely inexpensive and worthwhile but time-consuming mechanisms for smaller enterprises to connect, collaborate, ally, and learn from each other?
- Business telecenters should offer so much more than e-mail and Internet access. But do they? What are the specific services that telecenters could offer?
- What should be included in your country's e-commerce strategy? How can a National Advisory Board promote awareness of electronic commerce?

Key E-Commerce Programs and Services

This section is designed to help your strategy designers and key decision-makers organize the specific areas in which you would like to focus your strategy. It addresses two spheres of concern. The first is for the sectoral sphere (e.g., agro-business and automotive components). The second is the information and communications technology sphere (e.g., call center services, back office, logistical support, software integration and development, manufacturing and export of electronics and computer hardware manufacturing, development of a Silicon Alley and specific e-commerce enterprises).

Real Needs

If the Internet is to truly become the goose that lays golden eggs, much more research and assessment of needs must be undertaken. We must determine the real software needs of enterprises to improve customer service, billing and invoicing, order processing and the myriad of other processes that businesses need to automate using technology. We don't urgently need to download Web pages on our cell phones (at least I don't think so), but we do need to understand the practical applications of all technology that will make use more efficient and effective. Computer manufacturers, software designers, and cell phone providers continue to develop technology . . . but is it really what we want and need?

New Technology

Developers of new technology should be encouraged to develop technology that responds to the consumer's need, rather than pressing us to adopt high tech and irrelevant gadgets and gizmos. Just review the list software companies that cannot make a profit. Or review the "dot.bomb" Internet companies that were highly leveraged by investors, but were unable to respond to consumer and buyer needs.

Sources of Assistance

Of course, businesses need a neutral and competent provider of advice through in-person and online counseling, establishment of e-commerce telecenters that do more than provide access to e-mail, a volunteer e-corps, and perhaps a model Web template for businesses. And is there not a niche to offer practical training programs that don't cost two thousand dollars a day?

Shared Learning

Does the small business development center or university in your community, or somebody else, host e-mail-based discussions for businesses to share ideas and learn from each other? Does your community offer e-commerce and call center incubators? Is there an online product directory of products and services available from your community? Can you submit your sites to a neutral organization for evaluation?

Guides

Can you find a legal guide for e-business, a roster of experts in e-commerce, an Internet search techniques manual, a guide on how to design, develop and maintain sites, and how to use online trade statistics in foreign market research? Probably not—because many organizations, universities, and agencies are accustomed to providing traditional counseling, training, and education. Certainly there are some "islands of excellence" or first movers who are keeping ahead of the e-commerce curve. However, the vast majority are not providing up-to-date consulting, training, or education.

What the Group Should Do: Programming

Meeting on a regular basis, the group should be able to identify and implement strategies and programs regarding the following:

- Improve and Build Information and Communication Technology Infrastructure. This can include programs such as efficient and timely deregulation of the telecommunications sector, convincing traditional telephone companies to build attractive rates for access to Internet lines in homes and office, offering Internet access centers, laying fiber optic cable, placing computers in schools and libraries, and building software technology parks.
- Identify Key Policy and Enabling Legislation Needed. A listing of specific policies and laws will ensure the legality of electronic contracts, recognition of digital signatures, and prevention and punishment of computer crimes and any other concerns identified by the group.
- Address Regulatory and Security Issues. When identifying programs and services under this area, the group will be able to determine if a national certifying authority for digital signatures has been created, if secure online banking has been or will be provided for, etc.
- Define Programs to Encourage Public/Private Partnerships and Network Building. What has been done to create a network of groups seeking to develop comprehensive, coordinated, and synergistic programs on e-commerce? Who are the e-commerce experts, and has a roster of them been prepared?
- Create Programs to Foster Greater Awareness Among Businesses. What are the programs, seminars, or services that have

been developed to create greater knowledge and awareness about e-commerce among businesses? Some program ideas include designating a specific year as the Year of E-Commerce, launching an awareness building campaign, educating the media, launching a volunteer e-corps, etc. Other examples are a specialized program that can match exporters and importers of fresh fruit and vegetables, profile successful service export strategies, offer online exhibitions of products from indigenous firms, and provide answers to the most commonly asked questions regarding e-commerce constraints.

- Needs Assessments and Other Surveys. Training institutes, technical colleges and universities should identify what, if any, a broadly-based assessment of enterprise, supplier, and buyer needs they are undertaking and/or have completed. Trainers and educators are beginning to develop programs to understand better the actual costs of e-commerce, understand success factors and barriers to e-commerce, and to research buyer, supplier and consumer psychology. What other kinds of technical research are being conducted or contemplated?

- Counseling and Training Programs. This section should include a number of initiatives that have already been undertaken, such as online counseling or one-on-one counseling by experts and training on all the various aspects of electronic commerce. It should also list initiatives that should be undertaken at some specific time(s) in the future.

- Other Technical Programs. Online discussions, e-mailing of trade leads, creation of e-commerce or call center incubators, national online product directories, assistance with site design, registration of enterprises under a national domain system, e-commerce case studies, and online sector auctions are just a few of the programs and services that could be offered.

- Guides and Periodicals. What are the best books, guides, and magazines that have been published on e-commerce strategy, market research, online marketing and communication, legal, policy and regulatory aspects, security and encryption, financial issues, how to build customer-responsive sites, and technical issues? Where can they be assembled and used?

- Financing and Grant Programs. Some communities may want to offer e-commerce project grants, micro loans for purchase of computers and Web design, duty free import of computers, a technology research fund, and subsidized access to the Internet. What are the current programs to help finance and reduce costs associated with e-commerce?

Bridging the Counseling, Training, and Education Divide?

Here is what others have done to bridge the divide. In 2000 and 2001, I conducted an international survey of export development organizations in order to identify the specific programs and services offered by a particular country. As a result, 11 key programmatic areas were identified as being an appropriate focus for program and service delivery by the private sector, consulting firms, universities, and government agencies. Under each of these categories, specific programs and services have been identified as being important to the full development of e-commerce in a country.

- *Programs to Improve and Build ICT Infrastructure*
  Offer Internet access centers
  Lay fiber optic cable
  Place computers in all schools and libraries
  Build software technology parks

- *Programs to Identify Key Policy and Enabling Legislation*
  Ensure legality of electronic contracts
  Ensure legal recognition of digital signatures
  Adopt asymmetric crypto system/hash function and e-money
      systems
  Ensure prevention and punishment of computer crimes

- *Programs to Address Regulatory and Security Issues*
  Create certifying authority
  Create a repository of digital signature certificates
  Ensure, facilitate, and educate about online banking
  Establish payment gateways
  License Internet service providers

- *Programs to Encourage Public/Private Partnerships and Network Building*
  Create a national network of organizations on e-commerce

Create a virtual community of organizations for networking/
   information sharing
Develop a national roster of experts in e-commerce/team of
   e-business advisors
Establish a national e-commerce task force to develop a
   national strategy
Appoint a national e-commerce coordinating and
   implementation committee
Appoint an e-envoy and coordinator for private sector
   involvement
Develop a network of procurement agencies
Offer PRO-NET (Procurement Network)
Offer ACE NET (Investors' Network)
Offer mentor-protégé linkages

- *Programs to Create Greater Awareness Among Businesses and
   Government Decision Makers*
   Show how e-commerce is changing small business
   Designate a year as the Year of E-Commerce
   Offer a national e-commerce awareness week
   Launch an awareness-building campaign
   Create awareness-building tools such as flyers and posters
   Raise awareness among youth and young parents
   Launch a media education campaign/form a business media
      advisory council
   Target sectors for B2B growth
   Launch a computer literacy campaign
   Offer informational street kiosks
   Provide public Internet terminals for Internet and e-mail access
   Provide an e-mail address for every business
   Launch a volunteer e-corps
   Create e-mail marketing and communication lists
   Focus on e-commerce for women entrepreneurs

- *Research Programs to Better Understand Enterprise E-Commerce Needs*
   Understand the true costs of Internet commerce
   Determine the best mechanisms to ensure secure transactions
   Create an e-commerce scorecard to understand factors/barriers
      impeding success
   Understand buyer, supplier, and consumer psychology

Research methods to reduce conflict with traditional buying practices

- *Needs Assessment Surveys to be Undertaken*
  Undertake an assessment of enterprise/supplier needs
  Undertake an assessment of buyer needs
  Undertake a research campaign
  Identify software needs of smaller enterprises
  Develop a software evaluation program
  Determine return on investments in Web Site

- *Counseling and Training Programs*
  Offer e-mail/online counseling and online answer desks
  Provide online commercial documentation
  Create a national portal for business
  Develop sector-specific portals and sector-specific training
  Develop a Web site template to offer smaller enterprises
  Offer an e-commerce training program for businesses and degree program for students
  Offer Internet research training

- *Other Technical Programs*
  Offer online discussions
  E-mail trade leads
  Create e-commerce incubators
  Create call center incubators
  Develop a national online product directory/virtual trade shows/online showroom
  Evaluate Web sites
  Provide assistance with Web site design
  Provide cost reimbursement for Web site design
  Register enterprises under a national domain system
  Offer an e-commerce case study competition with universities
  Organize online sector auctions (e.g., coffee auctions)
  Improve online trade information services

- *Financing and Cost-Reduction Schemes*
  Offer e-commerce project grants
  Offer micro loans for purchase of computers and Web site design
  Offer duty-free import of computers

Offer a technology research fund

Offer reduced/subsidized Internet access charges

Offer a "One Computer per Family" campaign

Offer incentives for investment and competition within sectors

Offer financial rewards for best Web sites

Provide tax credits for e-commerce business

Offer preferential rates on subscribing to fiber optic cable

It's All about Who's Going to Do What

As a thought leader, what will you do to help businesses become e-savvy? What are your tax dollars doing to help you? How can the private and public sector join hands to take advantage of the potential technology and Internet present? But how will organizations develop partnerships, encourage networking and awareness building, conduct research and assess needs, offer consulting, training, and publications, and advocate on behalf of businesses in your community?

For many communities as well as whole countries, information technology, the Internet, and e-commerce are viewed as "the most democratizing forces on earth today," and as "tools that can let us achieve our dream of being prosperous" (from a summary of a developing country's national e-commerce strategy).

Let there be no mistake: The majority of developed and developing countries view e-commerce as their golden opportunity to finally compete in the world market. As a result, complex and aggressive public and private sector plans are being developed to use e-commerce as the primary tool for growth and expansion. Each community, each country must ask itself, "What are we doing to respond to the opportunities presented by the Internet? What are the specific programs and services that can be developed to help smaller enterprises to find new buyers and suppliers, and to use the Internet to improve efficiencies and expand client outreach?"

And this question is especially important for organizations such as local chambers of commerce, US Department of Commerce, US Small Business Administration and their Small Business Development Centers, universities, and other "developers" of smaller business. The private market is filled with missed opportunities, competing technologies, and inadequate education, training and media coverage—which mean confusion for millions of enterprises.

Certainly many in the United States feel that the "market" will adjust, identify winners, educate, and create more successful businesses. Others believe that the US is "so far ahead" of other countries, that there is no need for a coordinated effort at the local, state, and national level to provide sound education and training to US enterprises.

However, if counseling does not get better, if training remains expensive and not practical, if educators do not educate themselves on the practical aspects of the new economy, if relevant research is not undertaken and acted upon, the e-commerce economy will remain the domain of large businesses. Yes, make no mistake: other countries have created and will continue to create a more prosperous environment for their smaller businesses to survive and thrive in the electronic economy.

But the question remains: what are you, as a thought leader in your community, government agency, as an educator, student, consultant, technology developer, Web designer, ISP, or legal expert going to do to help achieve these goals?

All communities want to:

- Provide high-speed Internet access.
- Protect consumers.
- Accelerate the spread of e-commerce.
- Broaden understanding of the impact of e-commerce.
- Develop strategies to help enterprises overcome barriers to the use of the Internet.
- Ensure a global free flow of e-commerce.
- Protect patentable inventions.
- Privatize the domain name system.
- Ensure that no new taxes are imposed on electronic transactions.
- Develop a uniform commercial legal framework that recognizes, facilitates, and enforces electronic transactions world-wide.
- Develop privacy codes.
- Oppose efforts by foreign governments to impose standards or to use standards for e-commerce as non-tariff trade barriers.
- Monitor newly developing experiments in electronic payment systems.
- Ensure reliable and secure telecommunications.
- Expand procurement opportunities.

Model Strategy Documents

Some model national, regional, state, and local e-commerce strategies can be found on the Internet or by sending an e-mail to the following:

Australia: http://www.austrade.gov.au/EXPORTINGONLINE/
Page51476.asp

Australia: http://www.noie.gov.au/projects/ecommerce/SME/
index.htm

Canada: http://e-com.ic.gc.ca/english/60.html

Canada: http://www.e-com.ic.gc.ca/

European Union: http://europa.eu.int/pol/emu/index-en.htm

Ireland: http://www.entemp.ie

Jordan: raed.bilbessi@intaj.net

Slovenia: Mojca.Osojnik@gzs.si

Sweden: http://www.naring.regeringen.se/pressinfo/
infomaterial/pdf/n2000_076en.pdf

http://www.naring.regeringen.se/pressinfo/infomaterial/pdf/n200
0_075en.pdf

http://www.naring.regeringen.se/pressinfo/infomaterial/pdf/n200
0_073en.pdf

South Africa: http://www.ecomm-debate.co.za/greenpaper/
greenpaper.PDF

Note: Many URLs are no longer active. Refer to www.archive.org.

Your Report

To recap what has been mentioned throughout this chapter, your report should include:

- *Introduction:*
  Include the members of the group and the underlying goals in preparing the strategy and how the strategy was prepared.

- *Programming:*
  Include descriptions of the programs, responsible implementing organization(s), human resources needed, physical assets needed, and expected date of completion.

- *Budget:*
  Outline the estimated financial needs for each program and sources for the financing.

While the contents of your strategy document should remain flexible in light of new information, those are the basic elements that you should incorporate.

The Report as a Tool

Once the first edition of your report is prepared, it should be distributed and promoted widely to individual members of the groups that were represented in the coalition. By asking for—and obtaining—their support and involvement, you will expedite what you wish to achieve from your efforts. These issues of infrastructure, training and education, enabling legislation, research, technology advancement, and financing are urgent. Moreover, when individual firms, associations and government bodies have the report, it will spur them on to become involved—or better involved—with e-commerce now, to their own benefit.

9

The Future of E-Commerce for Developing Countries

Of course, all of the information, suggestions and comments in the preceding chapters for enterprises, associations, and governments apply to those in developing countries as well.

Yet, developing countries face unique conditions. If firms and associations are to succeed in e-commerce as sellers as well as buyers, they must engage their peers and government policy-makers in some fundamental planning, practices, and provisioning to overcome difficulties, while at the same time work together to gain all the possible benefits from their comparative advantages.

Because of the Internet's global nature, firms in developing countries *will* receive queries and orders from underdeveloped countries and must be prepared to deal with them. As discussed earlier, as the Internet becomes even more widespread within these countries, it would be shortsighted, if not downright foolish, for firms to ignore the potential there, for developing countries, too, have access to the Internet and great room to expand.

As Samli points out in this book, *Entering and Succeeding in Emerging Countries: Marketing to the Forgotten Majority*[1], "catering to the forgotten majority . . . is also very profitable. . . . In a decade or so, the forgotten majority will start asserting itself so that it will not remain forgotten." He also maintains that this market "is likely to grow faster than the industrialized markets of the world."

Let's take a closer look at some of these conditions and issues. First, however, note the comments by Nicklas Lundblad,[2] CEO Stockholm Chamber of E-commerce, that put several issues regarding the digital divide into perspective:

Exhibit 9.3 ICT and E-Commerce Indicators

	Telephone Mainlines Per 1000 People	Personal Computers Per 1000 People	# of Secure ISPs* Servers	Annual GDP	% Growth
Canada	655	360	425	4530	1.6
Chile	149	36	21	112	–1.1
Colombia	160	34	8	54	–4.3
Indonesia	29	9	1	4	5.6
Malaysia	203	69	24	8	5.8
Mexico	112	44	23	3	3.5
Singapore	482	437	267	483	5.4
South Africa	125	55	33	470	1.2
Trin. & Tobago	216	54	28	8	6.8
Thailand	86	23	5	103	4.2
Uganda	3	3	1	1	4.4
United States	844	81	563	200	2.3
Vietnam	27	9	0	4	5.6

Source: World Development Indicators Database, World Bank Group, 2001.
*Internet Service Providers.

as US$75 per month compared to US$10 in the United States and US$15 in the United Kingdom. Considering the low levels of income in Africa (South Africa has the highest annual per capita income in Africa at a rate of US$3151), subscription charges are prohibitive and beyond the reach of most enterprises. Further, the cost of local or long-distance telephone calls giving access to the Internet are usually significantly higher in developing countries.

Lack of Equipment

According to the World Trade Organization (WTO),[3] the personal computer ratio per 100 inhabitants gives an indication of the size of the information technology gap. The figure ranged in 2002 from 18 for high-income countries such as in the United States to 2.3 for medium-income countries and 0.1 for low-income countries.[4] The lack of effective and contemporary equipment seriously hinders the development of global e-commerce.

Are we creating a digital divide between the haves and have-nots of electronic commerce? If so, what is the nature of this divide? What is it that leaves us divided? These are important issues to answer to ensure that we utilize the new technologies to balance and strengthen developing countries and developed countries alike.

There are a number of points that deserved to be made in discussing the digital divide.

Firstly, we must ask what the digital divide consists of. What exactly is it that is dividing us? I think that it would be a mistake here to focus on hardware, and to use the number of computers in any given country as the only measure of that country's technological advancement. In many cases what have been products are becoming services, and, therefore, developing countries may very well reap the benefits of the new technologies without massive investments in hardware. E-commerce, for example, can often be introduced as an application service provider utility in countries where the hardware infrastructure is weaker than it is in some developed countries. This will eliminate the need for heavy investments in hardware and also allow for quicker deployment of the new technologies, which will, in turn, lead to the growth needed to deploy hardware as seems reasonable. If we focus on the number of computers we will fail to realize that the services are the true value-adding part of any information system.

Secondly, it is important to see that the cost for bridging the digital divide is much less than the cost of bridging, say, the medical divide. The digital divide is a problem that we can efficiently address and cure—but many of the other divides that the world suffers from are harder to rectify.

Thirdly, the digital divide consists in a knowledge gap, as much as in a hardware or access gap. Education is the prime factor in eliminating this divide, and this also makes the digital divide different from, say, the medical divide—since the latter is dependent on equipment and medicines to a much higher degree.

Fourthly, there is much to be gained from bridging the digital divide. The resulting markets will necessarily be more diversified and competitive, and this will in turn open up for a continued globalization of knowledge, markets and democracies. The digital divide is not the result of the globalization process, but the globalization process—at least when it comes to information infrastructure going global—will result in a greater equality in the distribution of access and knowledge of digital technologies.

E-commerce can and will be a driving factor in all this. Today this might seem more like science fiction than hard facts, but it is not. The economics of bridging the digital divide are sound. Leaving half the world behind is not the rational choice.

The digital divide must not be allowed to become a concept that demonises the technological development, however. We must realise that divides reflect a time lag in the spread and adoption of technologies, and not a static and constant distribution of access and knowledge about these technologies. The only way of overcoming the digital divide is accelerating the process of technological development and adoption. I sincerely believe that we will then see new patterns emerge, and I hope that these patterns will be evidence of not a digital divide, but rather of a digital bridge across the troubled waters of our world and economies.

Conditions and Issues: *Internet Access*

Access to the Internet and its array of goods, services, and information is growing rapidly, as Exhibit 9.1 shows.

The potential for even more people to begin using the Internet around the globe for business education, international trade, international communication, international marketing, and actual online transactions is vast. Consider, for example, the percentage of Internet users in just a few countries from 1998 through 2000, as shown in Exhibit 9.2.

Market for the ICT Sector/E-Commerce

Clearly, while great strides have been made, there is vast opportunity in all countries to increase the number of telephone lines, personal computers, ISPs, and secure servers.

Consider the telecommunication and equipment market by country for the year 2000, indicated in Exhibit 9.3. Certainly challenges,

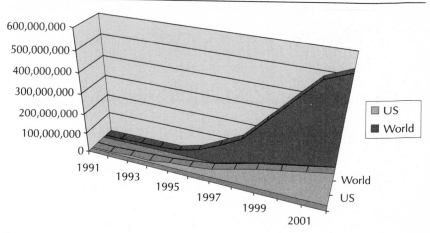

EXHIBIT 9.1 Estimated Number of Internet Users, 1991–2002

Source: Jupiter Media Metrix.

EXHIBIT 9.2 Percentage of Internet Users from 1998 through 2000 (figures have been rounded)

Country	1998	1999	2000
Canada	15	42	43
Malaysia	1	3	7
Mexico	1	1	3
Singapore	15	42	43
South Africa	3	4	4
Tunisia	1	1	1
Venezuela	1	1	2

Source: McCue.

competitive advantages, and disadvantages exist in the ICT and e-commerce market.

Connectivity Cost

The connectivity challenge faced in developing countries is even greater. The average cost to access the Internet through a dial-up connection in Africa in 2002 is quoted by the International Telecommunications Union

Are we creating a digital divide between the haves and have-nots of electronic commerce? If so, what is the nature of this divide? What is it that leaves us divided? These are important issues to answer to ensure that we utilize the new technologies to balance and strengthen developing countries and developed countries alike.

There are a number of points that deserved to be made in discussing the digital divide.

Firstly, we must ask what the digital divide consists of. What exactly is it that is dividing us? I think that it would be a mistake here to focus on hardware, and to use the number of computers in any given country as the only measure of that country's technological advancement. In many cases what have been products are becoming services, and, therefore, developing countries may very well reap the benefits of the new technologies without massive investments in hardware. E-commerce, for example, can often be introduced as an application service provider utility in countries where the hardware infrastructure is weaker than it is in some developed countries. This will eliminate the need for heavy investments in hardware and also allow for quicker deployment of the new technologies, which will, in turn, lead to the growth needed to deploy hardware as seems reasonable. If we focus on the number of computers we will fail to realize that the services are the true value-adding part of any information system.

Secondly, it is important to see that the cost for bridging the digital divide is much less than the cost of bridging, say, the medical divide. The digital divide is a problem that we can efficiently address and cure—but many of the other divides that the world suffers from are harder to rectify.

Thirdly, the digital divide consists in a knowledge gap, as much as in a hardware or access gap. Education is the prime factor in eliminating this divide, and this also makes the digital divide different from, say, the medical divide—since the latter is dependent on equipment and medicines to a much higher degree.

Fourthly, there is much to be gained from bridging the digital divide. The resulting markets will necessarily be more diversified and competitive, and this will in turn open up for a continued globalization of knowledge, markets and democracies. The digital divide is not the result of the globalization process, but the globalization process—at least when it comes to information infrastructure going global—will result in a greater equality in the distribution of access and knowledge of digital technologies.

E-commerce can and will be a driving factor in all this. Today this might seem more like science fiction than hard facts, but it is not. The economics of bridging the digital divide are sound. Leaving half the world behind is not the rational choice.

The digital divide must not be allowed to become a concept that demonises the technological development, however. We must realise that divides reflect a time lag in the spread and adoption of technologies, and not a static and constant distribution of access and knowledge about these technologies. The only way of overcoming the digital divide is accelerating the process of technological development and adoption. I sincerely believe that we will then see new patterns emerge, and I hope that these patterns will be evidence of not a digital divide, but rather of a digital bridge across the troubled waters of our world and economies.

Conditions and Issues: *Internet Access*

Access to the Internet and its array of goods, services, and information is growing rapidly, as Exhibit 9.1 shows.

The potential for even more people to begin using the Internet around the globe for business education, international trade, international communication, international marketing, and actual online transactions is vast. Consider, for example, the percentage of Internet users in just a few countries from 1998 through 2000, as shown in Exhibit 9.2.

Market for the ICT Sector/E-Commerce

Clearly, while great strides have been made, there is vast opportunity in all countries to increase the number of telephone lines, personal computers, ISPs, and secure servers.

Consider the telecommunication and equipment market by country for the year 2000, indicated in Exhibit 9.3. Certainly challenges,

Exhibit 9.1 Estimated Number of Internet Users, 1991–2002

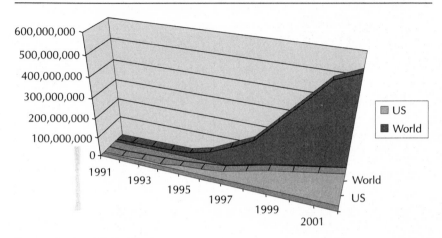

Source: Jupiter Media Metrix.

Exhibit 9.2 Percentage of Internet Users from 1998 through 2000 (figures have been rounded)

Country	1998	1999	2000
Canada	15	42	43
Malaysia	1	3	7
Mexico	1	1	3
Singapore	15	42	43
South Africa	3	4	4
Tunisia	1	1	1
Venezuela	1	1	2

Source: McCue.

competitive advantages, and disadvantages exist in the ICT and e-commerce market.

Connectivity Cost

The connectivity challenge faced in developing countries is even greater. The average cost to access the Internet through a dial-up connection in Africa in 2002 is quoted by the International Telecommunications Union

EXHIBIT 9.3 ICT and E-Commerce Indicators

	Telephone Mainlines Per 1000 People	Personal Computers Per 1000 People	# of Secure ISPs* Servers	Annual GDP	% Growth
Canada	655	360	425	4530	1.6
Chile	149	36	21	112	−1.1
Colombia	160	34	8	54	−4.3
Indonesia	29	9	1	4	5.6
Malaysia	203	69	24	8	5.8
Mexico	112	44	23	3	3.5
Singapore	482	437	267	483	5.4
South Africa	125	55	33	470	1.2
Trin. & Tobago	216	54	28	8	6.8
Thailand	86	23	5	103	4.2
Uganda	3	3	1	1	4.4
United States	844	81	563	200	2.3
Vietnam	27	9	0	4	5.6

Source: World Development Indicators Database, World Bank Group, 2001.
*Internet Service Providers.

as US$75 per month compared to US$10 in the United States and US$15 in the United Kingdom. Considering the low levels of income in Africa (South Africa has the highest annual per capita income in Africa at a rate of US$3151), subscription charges are prohibitive and beyond the reach of most enterprises. Further, the cost of local or long-distance telephone calls giving access to the Internet are usually significantly higher in developing countries.

Lack of Equipment

According to the World Trade Organization (WTO),[3] the personal computer ratio per 100 inhabitants gives an indication of the size of the information technology gap. The figure ranged in 2002 from 18 for high-income countries such as in the United States to 2.3 for medium-income countries and 0.1 for low-income countries.[4] The lack of effective and contemporary equipment seriously hinders the development of global e-commerce.

Telecommunication Infrastructure

Also according to the WTO, the level of telecommunication infrastructure in developing countries is highly diverse. The gap between developed and developing countries in general remains significant. Using teledensity (main lines per 100 inhabitants) as an indicator, the figure in 2002 for developed countries was more than 48, around 10 for middle income countries, and around 1.5 for lesser developed countries. Certainly access to basic telephonic services remains a prerequisite for electronic commerce. Yet some 2 billion people have never seen a telephone and the vast majority of people in the developing world do not have a telephone within a walking distance of their homes.[5]

Limited access is exacerbated by the weaknesses of networks, affecting the quality and reliability of communication as well as a huge gap in telecommunication infrastructure between urban and rural areas in developing countries.

Couple this with the monopoly state or privately run telecommunication carriers who do not necessarily want consumers to have easy and cheap access to the Internet. This is because of the potential impact on their bottom lines. Moreover, some governments restrict what their citizens can access. Is there any wonder why e-commerce is not a global phenomenon—yet?

Limited Connectivity

In 2002, just more than 163 million people were connected to the Internet—fewer than three percent of the people in the world.[6] And while Canada and the United States have more than 55 percent of the online population, Africa, with nearly twice the population of North America, had 0.7 percent of its population online.

Certainly, the number of e-mail services from walk-in telecenters and cybercafes, which are more prevalent in some developing countries than in developed ones, may underestimate the extent to which those in developing countries have access to the Internet. Nevertheless, the number of businesses in developing countries with an online presence is minuscule.

Furthermore, Exhibits 9.3 and 9.4 show the interrelated nature of connectivity, computers, and e-commerce providers.

As pointed out in the section on networking in Chapter 8, government agencies, nonprofit organizations, and national associations, etc., in developing countries must also grapple with a number of financial,

EXHIBIT 9.4 Estimated Number of People Online with Access at Home and at Work

Region	Number (millions)	Percentage
Total Online, World	163.25	100.0
Africa	1.14	0.7
Asia/Pacific	26.97	16.5
Europe	38.55	23.6
Middle East	0.88	0.5
Canada & USA	90.63	55.5
South America	5.26	3.2

Source: International Telecommunications Union, 2001.

legal, connectivity, and other policy issues related to e-commerce. These include issues of encryption, security of payments, taxation, certification and authentication, confidentiality, intellectual property protection, fraud and consumer protection, and access to telecommunications. Such a national e-commerce strategy must also address how the Internet will benefit enterprises, foster an awareness and appreciation among enterprises of what the Internet is, provide answers to technical questions, and train enterprises on how to use the Internet as a sales, marketing, communication, and supply management medium.

Important exchanges of information and other efforts are taking place in developing countries. Profiled here are "cut-in" suggestions, and what has been happening in Azerbaijan.

Great Leap Forward? E-Commerce Strategies in Developing Countries

By Dr. Wenli Wang, independent e-commerce consultant, wenli@ wenli.net

> The Internet provides the common ground for global commerce in such an efficient and responsive manner never imagined before. Each nation is now facing challenges about how to leverage the Internet and the new economy. While e-commerce leaders, such as the US, Germany, Japan, and

Finland, continue seeking sustainable e-business models and growth, developing countries are looking for the right e-commerce strategies that fit with the global economics and culture of their own.

Take China as an example. By June 30, 2004, China's Internet users totaled 87 million, according to People's Daily Online (www.english.people.com/CN/20040811_152529.html) and this number is expected to increase four-fold within two years, the Internet usage in China is still mainly for communication rather than commerce. B2C in China hardly reaches high-degree economies of scale because there is not yet an efficient and compatible online payment system. B2B needs to be built mostly from scratch; there are hardly any digitized assets in most domestic businesses. This offers certain advantages—there is no need for these businesses to deal with legacy information systems—and challenges—many other developing countries have these advantages too and are also seeking ways to place their nations strategically in the new order of the global economy.

Hence, the main challenge for developing countries in adopting e-commerce is to choose the best fit among the technologies and business models that have proven successful in developed countries or even those innovative ideas that have not been practiced yet. For example, a nation without a domestically compatible credit card payment system can make a great leap forward to implement nationwide digital money systems directly; a nation without barcode-based inventory control systems can invest in a Radio Frequency Identification (RFID) system and even implement it ahead of developed countries; a nation without traditional UPS/FedEx drop boxes on street corners can directly build ATM-like kiosks that enable mailings, payments, and even pickups.

Finding the right cut-in points is critical, and this has been in the mind of many strategic decision-makers in underdeveloped countries. To do so, a thorough understanding of the pros and cons of existing technologies and models as well as insights into future development trends are necessary. For a nation to be profitable in the global new economy, its decision-makers have to think globally and innovatively first.

E-Commerce and ICT in a Developing Country: The Case of Azerbaijan

By Adil Baguirov, eBusiness consultant, MIPC/MMNK, adil@mmnk.org

Despite many difficulties—such as close to a million refugees, unresolved war, and occupation of close to 20 percent of territory, blockades, typical post-Soviet economic collapse, and an unpredictable internal political situation—the Internet has made its victorious entry into Azerbaijan by the mid 1990's and was readily adopted by a well-educated population (benefited by a 99 percent literacy rate). The first sites in this nation of 8 million were created in 1995, with the first e-commerce enabled sites and e-auctions appearing in 2000. Government has been actively contributing by spearheading Web development for its ministries and agencies and establishing an ICT office to coordinate the activities under the auspices of the Council of Ministers. Experiences of developed countries are studied to learn from mistakes and adopt the best strategies. The Finance Ministry is spearheading an e-government initiative with the technical assistance from an American computer company. Many businesses are fervently creating sites with all the basic information about them and their products and services, the first step before establishing a virtual storefront.

It is estimated that it is 180 times cheaper to establish an e-presence for a year than to lease real estate in the capital Baku, and 120 times cheaper to create a site than to renovate an existing physical store. These savings are immediately passed on to the customers with an average 15 percent discount on all items and free delivery. Thus, the perennial promise of e-commerce—cheaper, faster, and better—seems to hold true. Despite such obvious financial successes, as well as increasing number of Internet users, shoppers, and proliferation of various convenient payment solutions, the market will remain limited because of poor telecommunication infrastructure, weak legislation, and other macro-factors that simply cannot keep up with demand for e-commerce, thus turning away potential customers.

Hence, we have a dilemma: what appears to work for

some countries, especially the developed West, may not suit lesser developed countries. The biggest differences between the West and the rest are a well-established infrastructure leading to a high Internet accessibility and penetration (e.g., telephone and fiber optic lines, satellite channels, broadband connections, Internet hosts, high computer ownership and literacy, and other factors); and resultant successful e-commerce. There are many reasons why Amazon was successful in the West, and why it would fail in developing countries.

Large state-owned enterprises in developing countries suffer from poor accounting, corporate governance, costly enterprise resource planning (ERP), little customer relationship management (CRM), etc. Since ICT is proven to reduce transaction costs and improve the bottom line, it will certainly reduce chronic corruption, rampant among developing states, due to an increased transparency and open bidding.

Western expertise can help more than the multi-billion aid packages for the developing countries. Assistance with technology education, primarily in computer science, and domestic ICT production will bring developing countries out of poverty and into the productive membership of the World Trade Organization.

Notes

1. Samli, A.Coskun, *Entering and Succeeding in Merging Countries: Marketing to the Forgotten Majority* (Mason, OH: Thomson-Texere, 2003).
2. Nicklas Lundblad, "Bridging the Digital Divide," Speech to the World Bank Group, April 5, 2001.
3. World Trade Organization, "E-Commerce Indicators," World Development Indicator Database, 2001.
4. Ibid.
5. Ibid.
6. Ibid.

Afterword: Where Do We Go from Here?

In conclusion, I would like to offer my opinion on ways we can better use information and communication technologies to more quickly transform business, employees, and governments throughout the world.

More Seriously Consider How Information is Organized and Disseminated

Most importantly, I think we must more seriously discuss the ways in which business (and other) information is organized and disseminated—absolutely the most important determinants regarding to the extent to which not only e-commerce but e-education, e-health, and e-government will flourish. What groups select the information, how is it organized, and how is it disseminated? These are very powerful positions that will profoundly affect businesses, consumers, suppliers, and citizens who will increasingly rely on the Internet as their predominate source of information. For example, with 948,000 listings for "leather goods," there are several hundred thousand sites that this leather goods business is competing against to ensure they are found within the search listings.

Global Internet Sites Can Change the Thoughts and Actions of Millions

CNN, Google, Hotmail, and Yahoo therefore have the potential to be a very powerful force that could transcend ways that individuals have traditionally educated themselves, conducted business, and interacted with their government. Google receives well over 200 million hits per day to their Web site. In 2004, CNN received 33 million hits per day on a slow news day and 2.8 billion on a breaking news day. Yahoo, the 38th most recognized name in the world, received 237 million unique visitors to their portal site each month, and Hotmail drew 145 million people. The ability for organizations to communicate with millions around the globe in an instant is unprecedented in the history of mankind.

Consider if these global sites decide that they want to use their ability to directly communicate with millions of individuals, consumers, and citizens on a particular business, social, or political issue. These sites have the ability to change the thoughts and actions of millions of people around the globe. To me, this is so, so exciting but also very concerning because of the implications to international marketing, a country's culture, sovereignty to control access to information access, and traditional ways that governments create and limit economic opportunity for their citizens.

What is the UN's Role in Joining CNN, Google, Hotmail, and Yahoo as a Major Information Provider?

This is an important issue that should be more seriously considered by international non-profit and United Nations organizations. It is not in the business interest of CNN, Google, Hotmail or Yahoo to ensure that businesses in developing countries are found on the Internet as potential suppliers or sources of a particular product or service, or to ensure that people are receiving the information that will make a difference in their lives—but this is directly the business of these organizations, and therefore we must think more creatively and strategically about how we will use the Internet to communicate with and educate millions of people on a daily basis as effectively as these global sites do.

What Happens When Someone New to the Internet Goes Online?

We also need to consider what happens when individuals who have never been exposed to the Internet go online. They register for a free e-mail account with Yahoo and Hotmail or pay for one through a local ISP such as Africa Online. And where will they search for information to buy products and services or to educate themselves? According to a report Yahoo submitted to the White House in 2003 on the types of information people in developing countries are searching for, a surprising trend emerged: searches for entertainment, travel, and sports information far surpassed searches for health, education, business, government, environmental, or cultural content.

Entertainment and Travel Are the Most Popular Topics on Yahoo's Search Engine

For example, in Egypt, Israel, Jordan, Kuwait, Pakistan, and Saudi Arabia, the top three uses of Yahoo's search engine was for entertainment, travel, and personal finance. In Iran, the top three uses were entertainment, travel, and home decor. How to start a business, farming techniques, online education, trade opportunities, and vast other quests for self-education were glaringly missing from the users' search strings.

In India, according to Yahoo, the top 10 search words in September 2003 were for free e-mail access; news; Indian railways; wallpaper; cell phone ring tones; cricket; online greeting cards; astrology; chat, and finding jobs. To be sure, those affluent enough to access the Internet in India may not be concerned with self-improvement-related searches for information, but clearly the vast majority are not using the Internet for education, health, or business creation. But we have the means to change this.

E-Mail for All

I submit that if free e-mail portals were created for business, need-to-know information would be compiled in one central site that would be visited anytime a business checks his or her e-mail. This would be a much more cost effective and efficient way to direct individuals to finding business information (e.g., trade leads, new technology, financing sources, industry portals, etc.) that can help the business expand its electronic commerce. We must remember that several million brand new Internet users will come online in the next few years and several thousand of them will be conducting electronic commerce for the first time ever. These are people whose businesses we can improve if we are able to change their often casual quests for business information, leads, and opportunities into education and action. We need to think of new and innovative ways of communicating with and educating businessmen and businesswomen who are completely unaware of the Internet.

Creating a free e-mail portal is an effective way of communicating with businesses that have heretofore been unknown and unreachable— the almond grower in Turkey; the leather goods processor in Egypt; the printer in Bangalore. I'm talking about using the Internet to create new business opportunities with businesses that are usually not considered as potential business suppliers or buyers. We need to create a business place—a business portal—that can be considered as reliable a source for *business* information, education, and opportunities as Google and Yahoo have become.

Why Should We Care?

But first we should identify why we need to more critically think about how we can use technologies to foster greater commerce and electronic commerce. Simply put, based on the statistics presented below, we need to remember that thousands upon thousands of new businesses will be coming online and creating businesses in search of e-commerce as soon as they are connected. Consider, if you will, according to the International Telecommunications Union:

- As of 2003, just 0.4% of Africans and South Asians used the Internet compared to more than half the population in the US.
- In 2002, over seven million people were online in Africa, five million of whom were in South Africa. In 2004, 13.4 million people were online in Africa. Another ten million are expected to come online by the end of 2006.
- India's online population was 14 million in 2002; 21 million in 2003; 37 million in 2004; and is expected to top the 100 million mark in 2007.
- The number of Internet users globally was 385 million in 2000; 934 million in 2004; and is expected to be 1.35 billion in 2007.
- The percentage of Internet users worldwide was: Asia-Pacific, 34%; North America, 27%; Europe, 27%; Latin America, just over 10%; and Africa, 1.5%.
- In 2003, 3.2 million new Internet pages were created every 24 hours.

I find these statistics fascinating and yet ponderous. Clearly the creation and dissemination of information is booming but Latin America, Africa, and the Middle East are lagging behind. So, what can be done to bring greater connectivity, computers, and information to foster electronic commerce in the developing world?

What Can Be Done?

First and most importantly, we must create greater awareness of how to use the Internet for not only personal growth but business creation and e-commerce.

Next, we need to create a portal for *global* e-commerce that is as well-used as CNN, Google, Hotmail, and Yahoo.

Also, we need to encourage girls to use the Internet. The fact that 75% of the Internet users in the Middle East and 70% in Asia are boys should concern us all and spur us to encourage greater female use of the Internet.

We must train businesses on the applications of ICT. Thousands upon thousands of business managers in developing countries must be educated and trained on the use of ICT. We must work with the leading companies to create simple to understand, widely disseminated training programs that emphasize customer/citizen relationship management and systems integration, e-procurement, e-commerce, and e-government.

And as increasingly more government administrative functions, services, and information are provided using ICTs and the Internet, a new generation of government managers must be educated on e-gov fundamentals. Government managers must be able to draft technical contracts to create rather complex e-government systems that allow governments to better interact with citizens and for them to better manage internal administrative functions.

They also need to be familiar with technologies including servers, enterprise architectures, secure systems, electronic payments, and integrated database systems and networks, and know how to ask the techies to create effective citizen-centric profilers, search engines, and intelligent agents. Thousands around the globe are still adjusting to these new knowledge requirements and unfortunately we have not created adequate e-government or e-commerce programs that respond to their knowledge needs.

We need also to track the technology being created and confusing the marketplace because thousands of government managers and entrepreneurs throughout the world are attempting to create online systems but are woefully unaware of best practices, best technology, and best price, resulting in the wasting of millions of dollars in the creation of inadequate systems, thus severely limiting the growth of e-commerce and e-government in developing countries.

Recommendations for the World Summit on the Information Society

Following are excerpts from a journal article I wrote for *Harvard's Information Technologies and International Development** special education journal dedicated to opinions on the next summit. In it, I suggested five

*http://cyber.law.harvard.edu/wsis/list_by_author

The World Summit in Reflection: compendium of submissions collected by Information Technologies and International Development Journal, Berkman Center for Internet & Society at Harvard Law School, 2003 important next steps including determining how to finance the Solidarity Fund; immediately coalescing the private sector and building tangible and practical partnerships; surveying all 12,000 WSIS participants; coalescing a group of ICT experts to determine how to put more "e" in the UN; and identifying three to five urgent initiatives to be achieved by the summit.

At the next Summit, the Secretary General could launch initiatives that are already funded, organized, and proven as operational that address urgent and globally important issues such teaching girls to use the Internet; launching a free e-mail system for children in Africa and the Middle East; providing comprehensive e-governance and e-commerce training; launching an online global environmental monitoring system; etc.

We should form a shared vision on how to more efficiently and cost effectively use ICTs to address e-commerce, e-trade, e-government, e-health, e-education, and e-culture; using ICTs to respond to environmental, food distribution, and refugee crises, and the AIDS epidemic; how to use the Internet for information dissemination on business opportunities; and how to apply technology for greater efficiency and transparency within governments. Working through a representative group of individuals with expertise in ICT could help identify innovative ways to achieve global initiatives in these important areas.

I respectfully submit these are just a few of the practical things that can be and are being done to use information and communication technology for education and entrepreneurship. I don't see the glass as half empty or half full but overflowing with opportunity to truly use information and communication technologies to bring greater peace, prosperity, and education for all.

Glossary

AFNIC	Acronym for the French Association for Internet Naming & Cooperation
APNIC	Asia Pacific Network Information Center
Applet	Functionality applets provide independent mini-applications and content applets control navigation of a site, provide movement and minor functions.
Application	A self-contained program that executes well-defined tasks that the user controls
ASP	Application service provider
Backing up	The practice of making a copy of your computer documents onto tape or disc and storing these copies on a secure, off-site location
B2B	Business to business
B2C	Business to consumer
B2G	Business to government
CA	Certification authority who signs a digital identification certificate that verifies the connection between/among the contracting parties
CART	Constitutively Activated Receptor Technology
CGI	Common gateway interface
CPG	Consumer packaged goods
DES	Data Encryption Standard
DNS	Domain Name System
E-commerce	Doing business through the Internet, electronic commerce
EDI	Electronic Data Interchange
Electronic signature	An encrypted message that is legally joined to the main message. An independent CA holds the decryption key.
EQ	E-commerce quotient (similar to intelligence quotient, or IQ)
ERM	Employee Relationship Management
ERP	Enterprise Resource Planning
FAQ	Frequently Asked Questions—with answers

210

Frameset	The portion of a page that is "framed"
FTP	File Transfer Protocol
GSM	Global System for Mobile
GUI	Graphical User Interface
Hits	The number of visits to a Web site or page
HTML	Hyper Text Markup Language—language for the documents for the Web
HTTP	Hyper Text Transfer Protocol—protocol for transporting files from the server to the Web
ICANN	Internet Corporation for Assigned Names and Numbers
ICT	Information and Communications Technology
IDDN	International Deposit Digital Number
Information architecture	The structural system for arranging pages of information in squences
InterNIC 6	Internet Network Information Center regarding Internet domain name registration
IP	Internet Protocol
IRC	Internet Relay Chat
IT	Information Technology
ITC	International Trade Centre, Geneva (UNCTAD/WTO)
LOA	Linear Optical Amplifier
META tag	Identification of the key noun and one- or two-word descriptor ("key words") for the attention of search engines
MMS	Multimedia Messaging Service
'Net	The short form for Internet
NNTP	Network News Transfer Protocol
OECD	Organization for Economic Co-operation and Development
PC	Personal computer
PDA	Personal Digital Assistant
PRM	Partner Relationship Management
Reverse auction	You place your bid, the seller determines if it will accept it.
RFID	Radio Frequency Identification
RIPE-NCC	RIPE-NCC (RIPE Network Coordination Centre) for Europe. RIPE stands for Reseaux IP Europeens (European IP network).

SBDC	Small Business Development Center, administered by the US SBA
SET	Secure Electronic Transaction
SME	Small- to medium-size enterprises
Sockets	Endpoints in connections for passing data,
Spam	Unsolicited e-mail, usually sent to many e-mail addresses at once
Spamdexing	Using keywords frequently on a page in a futile attempt to get higher rankings with search engines.
Spider	A spider or robot is configured to follow the links in the Web from one page to another, usually one site at a time, much like a spider following the threads in its web.
SSL	The two-factor authentication and encryption protocol with the secure sockets layer protocol. "Layer" refers to the program elements between an application and the Internet.
SSM	Short Single Message
Supply chain	The firms involved in every step of production, from the smallest part to the completed product.
TCP/IP	Transmission control protocol/Internet Protocol-responsible for verifying the correct delivery of data from client to server to user
TLD	Top Level Domain
TRIPS	Trade-Related Aspects of Intellectual Property
UDDI	Universal Description, Discovery, and Integration, a white pages business directory and a technical specifications library
UN/CEFACT	United Nations Center for the Facilitation of Procedures and Practices for Administration, Commerce and Transport
UNCITRAL	United Nations Commission on International Trade Law
UNIDTROIT	Institute for the Unification of Private law
UDP	User Datagram Protocol
URL	Universal Resource Locator
US SBA	Small Business Administration, an agency of the United States government
VAT	Value Added Tax
VOIP	Voice Over Internet Protocol

Wi-Fi	Wireless fidelity—a means to connect to the Internet without cable
WIPO	World International Property Organization
WTO	World Trade Organization
WWW	World Wide Web
XHTML / XHTL	eXtensible HyperText Markup Language
XML	eXtensible Markup Language

Index

About the Author

Sarah McCue has been a manager and senior adviser to US government, World Bank, and United Nations organizations on trade development, e-commerce, e-government, and information and communication technology issues since 1990. Prior to joining the UN, she was state director of research for the Michigan Small Business Development Center at Wayne State University for eight years where she advised businesses on their foreign market entry strategies. She was president of the North American Association of Small Business Educators in 1998, and her six published books include the award-winning *Internet: Force or Farce?*; *Trade Secrets* (published in over 60 countries); and *Secrets of Electronic Commerce* (published in over 40 countries). She is founder of Women with 2020 Vision, an online mentoring program to teach girls entrepreneurial skills so that they might launch businesses in 2020 (www.womenwith2020vision.org), and The Remembering Site (www.TheRememberingSite.org) to record the online autobiographies of anyone anywhere. Her doctorate in international business and public adminstration is from Wayne State University.

About TEXERE

Texere, a progressive and authoritative voice in business publishing, brings to the global business community the expertise and insights of leading thinkers. Our books educate, enlighten, and entertain, and provide an intersection where our authors and our readers share cutting edge ideas, practices, and innovative solutions. Texere seeks to cultivate, enhance, and disseminate information that illuminates the global business landscape.

www.thomson.com/learning/texere

About the typeface

This book was set in 10 pt. Meridien. Meridien was created in 1957 for Deberny & Peignot by Adrian Frutiger of Switzerland. Frutiger based the design for his Meridien on the 16th century characters of Jenson. Meridien is a sharply cut typeface with triangular serifs and strongly contrasting thick to thin strokes.

Library of Congress Cataloging-in-Publication Data

McCue, Sarah S., 1967–
    Farce to force : building profitable e-commerce / Sarah S. McCue.
        p. cm.
    Includes bibliographical references and index.
    ISBN 0-538-72677-6 (alk. paper)
    1. Electronic commerce. 2. Electronic commerce—Management.
  3. Strategic planning. I. Title.
  HF5548.32.M3776 2005
  658.8′72—dc22

                                                    2005031440